Leadership Formation
in the African Context

Leadership Formation
in the African Context

Missional Leadership Revisited

SAMUEL DERESSA

Foreword by Gary M. Simpson

WIPF & STOCK · Eugene, Oregon

LEADERSHIP FORMATION IN THE AFRICAN CONTEXT
Missional Leadership Revisited

Resource Publications
An Imprint of Wipf and Stock Publishers
199 W. 8th Ave., Suite 3
Eugene, OR 97401

www.wipfandstock.com

PAPERBACK ISBN: 978-1-7252-9040-2
HARDCOVER ISBN: 978-1-7252-9041-9
EBOOK ISBN: 978-1-7252-9042-6

MARCH 23, 2022 9:20 AM

I dedicate this work to the memory of my mother Sarah Jorgo who was the first to form my faith.

CONTENTS

FOREWORD

RECOGNIZING THE REALITY OF global Christianity has set questions of mission and leadership on entirely different footings from those normalized according to paradigms set forth in the twentieth century.

With *Leadership Formation in African Context: Missional Leadership Revisited* Professor Samuel Yonas Deressa offers English reading audiences a dramatic investigation tutored through his own on-the-edge living as an African, Ethiopian Diasporal Christian currently residing and teaching in the United States. Deressa combines his experiential Diasporal moorings with the theological drama of social trinitarian reflection thus innovatively vexing three generally western lines of inquiry that have become too settled over the last quarter century: congregational studies, missional church ecclesiology, and missional leadership. He does this vexing by entering deeply into the leadership contexts, challenges, and learnings situated in four congregations of the Ethiopian Evangelical Church Mekane Yesus (EECMY) in Addis Ababa, Ethiopia.

Deressa cites John S. Mbiti's axiom, "Since I belong, therefore, I am, the *sine qua non* of existence" that identifies the core integrity of an African communal grounding of leadership, which moves missional leadership studies beyond the various western, Global North models of leadership still focused firmly through prisms of atomistic individualism. Further, Deressa's congregations demonstrate how the EECMY's long-standing commitment to holistic ministry complements, and indeed strengthens, the theological integrity of communally rooted leadership formation. Finally, Deressa takes special note how the Christian confession of the trinitarian nature of God binds together the various leadership formation practices of his four EECMY congregations and the contributions that this trinitarian confession offers to global Christianity in this new apostolic age of the Holy Spirit.

GARY M. SIMPSON
Emeritus, The Northwestern Lutheran Theological Seminary
Chair of Theology
Emeritus, Professor of Systematic Theology
Luther Seminary
St. Paul, MN, USA

ACKNOWLEDGMENTS

I would like to thank the many people without whose help and encouragement this book would not have been possible. First, my deepest gratitude goes to my thesis committee: Dr. Gary Simpson (thesis advisor), Dr. Mary Hess, and Dr. Paul Wee. I consider it a privilege indeed to have had each of you on my thesis committee. Dr. Simpson, I am deeply honored to thank you for your guidance and unmeasurable contribution to my theological thinking. I am also grateful to Dr. Alvin Luedke for feedback on chapters related to my qualitative study.

Thank you to the remarkable Luther Seminary community. I had wonderful years in which we shared special collegiality with many staff and students of the seminary. Thanks to the many professors from whom it was my honor to learn: Dr. Patrick Keifert, Dr. Dirk Lange, Dr. Mary Sue Dreier, Dr. Charles Amjad-Ali, Dr. Alvin, and Dr. Craig Van Gelder. Thank you also to special support I received from the International Students Office (Marie Hayes and Chenar Howard) during my studies.

I owe a debt of gratitude to my students and colleagues at Concordia University, St. Paul. I thank Dr. Paul Hillmer, the dean of Collage of Humanities and Social Science and Dr. Kavin Hall, vice President of Academic Affairs not only for their encouragement but for providing a resources that I needed to publish this book. I thank my colleagues in the theology department: Drs. Mark Koschmann, Heath Lewis, Reed Lessing, Mark Schuler, Joshua Hollmann, and our president Dr. Brian Friedrich.

I am thankful for the encouragement and support of many leaders of the Ethiopian Evangelical Church Mekane Yesus (EECMY): Rev. Yonas Yigazu, Lensa Gudina, and Aster Gudina, Dr. Bruk Ayele, Dr. Misga Mathewos, Rev. Iteffa Gobena, and Rev. Birhanu Ofgaha, and many more. I have received inspirational letters and phone calls from them that motivated me during my study. Many thanks also to leaders and members of the

Evangelical Lutheran Fellowship in North America. I have been blessed by being part of this fellowship in the last ten years.

Thanks also to the four congregation of the EECMY who allowed me to study their practices and interview their ministers, and who provided all kinds of documents cited in this research. I would like to thank all the research participants who contributed to sharing their meaningful experience with me. I also thank Fufa Ambacha, research director at Mekane Yesus Seminary, for helping me with translating, transcribing, and cross-checking the interviews.

Finally, my deepest thanks go to my wife Rebecca and three kids Ebba, Hawii and Abigail for their patience and encouragement over the past years. Finally, I am thankful to Karen Walhof and Dr. David Lump for proofreading parts of the manuscript.

List of Abbreviations

ALM	American Lutheran Mission
AUPM	American United Presbyterian Mission
BCMS	Bible Churchmen's Mission Society
BFBS	British and Foreign Bible Society
CCE	Coptic Church of Egypt
CEEC	Conference of Ethiopian Evangelical Churches
CMC	Church Missionary Society
GDP	Gross Domestic Product
DEM	Danish Evangelical Mission
EC-MY	Evangelical Church Mekane Yesus
EECMY	Ethiopian Evangelical Church Mekane Yesus
EEC	Eritrean Evangelical Church
EOC	Ethiopian Orthodox Church
FDRE	Federal Democratic Republic of Ethiopia
EPRDF	Ethiopian People Democratic Front
GHM	German Hermannsburg Mission
LWF	Lutheran World Federation
NetAct	Africa through Network for African Congregational Theology
NLM	Norwegian Lutheran Mission
OTR	Oromo Traditional Religion

LIST OF ABBREVIATIONS

SEM	Swedish Evangelical Mission
SIM	Sudan Interior Mission
SWOT	Strength, Weakness, Opportunity and Threat

LIST OF ILLUSTRATIONS

TABLES

FIGURES

Chapter 1

INTRODUCTION

As an African, I see myself as a product of a community where religion played a vital role in shaping the society. As a child, I was taught how to behave, worship, and relate to others in my community. Growing up, I observed how every member of the community was curiously watching over my shoulder, trying to shape my future to help me be someone who would meet their expectations. Through the years, I have come to understand that "belonging is the key to existence" in the African contexts: "since I belong, therefore, I am, the *sine qua non* of existence."[1] This is different from western contexts, where individualism has often taken the place of community.

As John Mbiti rightly articulates, the communities in Africa

> Make, create or produce the individual; for the individual depends on the corporate group. [According to African cultural world view], physical birth is not enough: the child must go through rites of incorporation so that it becomes fully integrated into the entire society. These rites continue throughout the physical life of the person, during which the individual passes from one stage of corporate existence to another.[2]

I have been through this cultural process to be who I am today. There is no doubt that there exists an intersection between the culture that

---

1. Mbiti, *African Religions and Philosophy*, 107.

2. Mbiti, *African Religions*, 141. As Samuel Maimela states, "[an] African is born, brought up, trained and led into maturity so as to attain and live the fullness of life undisturbed." See Maimela, "Traditional African Anthropology," 5.

nurtured my ethos and my faith. I have become aware that it was the culture that dictated my faith, and *vice versa*. The aim of this book is to explore such experiences by focusing on the study of congregational culture within which emerging leaders (like myself) are being formed and empowered in the African context. It explores the connection between two important concepts: spiritual formation and leadership formation.

Leadership formation continues to emerge today as one of the main topics discussed among scholars and church leaders. As the church faces massive shifts throughout the world, these scholars and leaders ask what it means to be a church and how to raise effective leaders in this new age. For churches in the Global North (the western world), the decline in membership of historical denominations, the growing number of migrates with diverse religious background, the rapid expansion of mega churches, and many other changes that are happening have resulted in the disruption of long-standing practices. Because of these shifts, there is a growing recognition among church leaders that business as usual is no longer possible, and that there needs to emerge a new or different alternative to what has been traditional leadership formation and practices.

In addition, global Christianity has experienced a major demographic shift in the past few decades. With the decline of Christianity in the North, and accelerated growth of Christianity in the South, the South has now become the heartlands of global Christianity. With this demographic shift, the Southern Christians have been aware of the need for missional leaders who can play a role in creating, shaping, and leading missional churches in global mission. This is mainly because, as Alan Roxburgh and Fred Romanuk have rightly stated, it is impossible to have a missional church or effectively engage in God's mission without missional leadership (and *vice versa*).[3] What does it mean to raise leaders in this new global age? How are disciples being formed in light of God's mission in the world? This book will address these questions by drawing mainly from the insights shared in the missional church literature to date, and attempts to contribute some new insights in to thinking further about leadership formation from African perspective.

3. Roxburgh and Romanuk, *Missional Leader*, 145.

MISSIONAL CHURCH CONVERSATION

The missional church conversation started in North America as a response to Leslie Newbigin's critical analysis of the missionary encounter in the 20th century. It was Newbigin's impression that the church in England had lost its connection with its cultural context that became the reason for the start of this conversation about mission. Newbigin, after working as a missionary in South India for a decade, came up with the following question: What is a missionary engagement with western culture in our time? Newbigin reflected much on Barth's idea of the Trinity and mission and its implications for the western context.

Challenged by Newbigin's writings, the missional church conversation was started in North America in the late 1980s. It was his identification and framing of crises and challenges in the way mission was understood and carried out in the western world that attracted American missiologists to engage in this conversation—which then resulted in the creation of the Gospel and Our Culture Network (GOCN). GOCN played a significant role in initiating and leading the conversation. This conversation mainly addressed ecclesiology and mission, with a focus on the dynamic inter-relations between gospel, church, and culture. As Guder and Barrett emphasized, this conversation was need to create a missional reorientation of theology, which is "the result of a broader biblical and theological awakening that had begun to hear the gospel in fresh ways."[4] They argue that this biblical and theological understanding originates from "God's character and purpose as a sending or missionary God [which] redefines our understanding of the Trinity."[5]

Since the first publication of the GOCN's *Missional Church: A Vission for the Sending of the Church in North America*, the term "missional" has been extensively used by scholars to talk about the identity and mission of the church.[6] Most of these publications are interested primarily in addressing the fundamental problems in American churches which are related to the notion that mission is an ecclesiastical activity—an activity of the church along with its other ministries. In previous years, mission was understood as either activities limited to local congregations or the sending

4. Guder and Barrett, *Missional Church*, 4–5.

5. Guder and Barrett, *Missional Church*, 5.

6. Roxburgh and Romanuk, *Missional Leader*; Van Gelder and Zscheile, *Missional Church in Perspective*, 17–40.

of missionaries to places outside the western world.[7] The concept of the missional church, on the other hand, introduced a theocentric reconceptualization of mission. In this way, the Trinity became the locus of mission. God is a missionary God inviting all people into communion with Him and with one another, and sending His people into the world to be involved in His ongoing creative work.[8] Therefore, as noted by Roxburgh and Romanuk, the missional church is defined as "a community of God's people who live into the imagination that they are, by their very nature, God's missionary people living as a demonstration of what God plans to do in and for all of creation in Jesus Christ."[9] The definition leads us to the understanding that the identity of the church is missional by its very nature.

The GOCN was, however, criticized for not including "real-life examples of congregations in the United States and Canada that were indeed missional."[10] In other words, the American and Canadian congregations were concerned with whether or not GOCN's articulation about missional church was reflected in the inner life and cultures of the congregations. In response to this concern, the GOCN formed a research team to study congregations in North America. The purpose of the research was to find models for the missonal church. The product of this research is the book *Treasures in Clay Jars: Patterns in Missional Faithfulness*.[11] The book explores the real-life expression of congregations "that are becoming missional."[12] In this book, the authors identified eight "patterns of missional faithfulness"[13] in the congregations they studied. This book, which is mainly about how emerging leaders are formed and empowered by cultures of congregations engaged in holistic ministry, follows a similar pattern but in a different context. It explores the leadership formation practice of one of the largest and the fastest growing Lutheran church in the world, the EECMY.

---

7. Bosch, *Transforming Mission: Paradigm Shifts in Theology of Mission*; Van Gelder, *The Ministry of the Missional Church*.

8. Van Gelder, *Ministry of the Missional Church*.

9. Roxburgh and Romanuk, *Missional Leader*.

10. Barrett, *Treasure in Clay Jars*, ix.

11. Barrett, *Treasure*, ix.

12. Barrett, *Treasure*, ix.

13. Barrett, *Treasure*, ix.

MISSIONAL LEADERSHIP CONVERSATION:
WHAT IS MISSING?

The missional church movement seeks to interpret leadership from the perspective of God's mission. Leadership is framed within the Trinitarian perspective, a perspective that is focused on the ongoing involvement of the Triune God in human history. Therefore, as rightly described by Roxburgh and Romanuk, missional leadership is "framed, understood, and articulated in relationship to the question of what God is doing in the world."[14] For them, this description about missional leadership leads one to the understanding that "leadership formation must be asked only in terms of what God is doing in forming the social community known as ecclesia."[15] In the last few decades, there has been a growing number of studies on the social nature of the Trinity. These studies have been used to frame church leadership.

While there has been much research conducted on the nature and identity of the missional church, few social scientific studies exist that address issues related to missional leadership.[16] These studies introduce the notion of missional leadership as the "ecclesiocentric default with its underlying anxiety for fixing the church."[17] Therefore, as Roxburgh contends, "the questions of what is at stake in forming missional leaders is still not being addressed."[18]

The other limitation in some research conducted on missional leadership is that they mainly focuses on "influence," the influence of a leader on their followers. Such an understanding of leadership echoes leadership theories developed in western individualistic culture where "I am" is more emphasized than "we are."[19] According to Roxburg and Romanuk,

14. Roxburgh and Romanuk, *Missional Leader*, 130.

15. Roxburgh and Romanuk, *Missional Leader*, 118.

16. For details about missional church conversation, see under "Definition of Key Terms" below and under the title "Missional Church" in Chapter 3.

17. Roxburgh, "Missional Leadership," 129.

18. Roxburgh, "Missional Leadership," 129.

19. For Alan Hirsch, for example, leadership should be understood as "a field that shape[s] behaviors." Hirsch, *Forgotten Ways*, 152. Terri Elton also focuses largely on a leader. For her, missional leadership "includes persons who understand their calling as disciples of Jesus Christ, see themselves as equipped by God with certain gifts, and believe that they are empowered by the Spirit to engage the world by participating in the creative and redemptive mission of God." Elton, "Charactoristics of Congregations," 178.

for example, "missional leadership is about creating an environment within which the people of God in a particular location may thrive."[20] This description works for them in a context where there exist "leaders with skills" who are able to create such an environment. A leader is at the center of their definition or description of missional leadership. As I have tried to explain above, however, such understanding of leadership is incompatible with African experience. Therefore, this book focuses on exploring the role of congregational (communal) cultures on the formation of emerging leaders (but not on the role of a single leader in shaping or forming the community).

The study of congregational cultures and their impact on leadership formation in the African context also requires us to go one step further and ask how leaders are formed in public space. In other words, besides the communal life of the congregations, what else contributes to the formation of emerging leaders? As Craig Van Gelder and Dwight Zscheile emphasize, missional leaders are formed and empowered "as faithful disciples through immersion not only in a vibrant, participating community where we learn from mature mentors in the faith, but also through [encountering] the lives of our neighbors and our world."[21] Joanna Collicutt also argues that "[leadership] formation is seen to involve the whole of a person's life—embodied thinking, feeling, acting and being in relationship [which] results in freedom."[22] What Collicutt refers to as "the whole of a person's life" is not merely an in-house (congregational) affair, but it includes "compassionate identification, participation, and companionship with those suffering under sin, oppression, injustice, exclusion, and despair."[23] However, due to less focus being given to the public character of the church, such aspects of leadership formation praxis have not been explored fully. This is the reason why Van Gelder and Zscheile argue that in the missional church

---

20. Roxburgh and Romanuk, *Missional Leader*, 6.

21. Van Gelder and Zscheile, *Missional Church*, 151.

22. Collicutt, *Psychology of Christian Character Formation*, 5.

23. Zscheile, "Missional Theology of Spiritual Formation," 19. Roger Helland and Leonard Hjalmarson also argue that leadership formation is related to "an attentive and active engagement of embodied love for God and neighbor expressed from the inside out." See Roger Helland and Leonard Hjalmarson, *Missional Spirituality*. See also the missional church conversation held at Luther Seminary on leadership formation. Van Gelder, *Missional Church and Leadership Formation: Helping Congregations Develop Leadership Capacity.*

conversation, issues related to "the public role of the church [still] needs further scrutiny."[24]

As we can see in the New Testament, the church is identified as *ekklesia*, a term that is used to describe the church as "a called-out public assembly,"[25] in contrast to spiritual movements characterized by a sense of calling generally limited to the private spheres. This term defines the very nature of the church and the context in which missional leaders are formed and empowered. Being sent by the Triune God, the church participates in a holistic mission that has its source, form, and goal in the Father's sending of the Son and the Son's sending of the Spirit into the world in order to participate in God's creation and redemption of the whole creation. As a community of believers, the church is called and sent by God to address the private as well as the public realms of life, and missional leaders are formed as a result. This is what I refers to in this book as *integral leadership formation* (see Figure 1 below). As shown in Figure 1 below, it is when congregations adopt a missional culture of holistic ministry in both their in-house and public engagement that their members experience *integral leadership formation.*

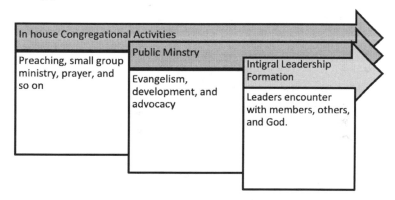

Figure 1: Integral Leadership Formation

The question is how one can study the cultures of congregations using such framework. The answer to this question is given in Nancy Ammerman et al.'s *Studying Congregations.* In this book, Ammerman et al. provide an outline on how to study the cultures of congregations, which include the

24. Van Gelder and Zscheile, *Missional Church in Perspective,* 140.

25. Van Gelder and Zscheile, *Missional Church in Perspective,* 140.

following: activities of the congregations (like rituals), artifacts (buildings, etc.), and stories told by the congregations (language, history, myths, world-views, theologies).[26] The main interest of this study is to use this framework and explore the cultures of EECMY congregations with the purpose of understanding how emerging leaders are being formed and empowered by it.

The study follows the rationale that there exists a correlation between a "philosophy of life" and "the nature of leadership" along with two interactive components, "theology of the church" and "cultural trends," which have an influence on both the life and leadership of the church.[27] The centrality of culture and its interconnectedness with economic, political, religious, and social change have become increasingly apparent in the emergence of indigenous leaders in the African context. Culture and development have always moved together.[28] As noted by Edgar Schein, it is also a reality that the "dynamic process of culture creation and management are the same essence of leadership and make one realize that leadership and culture are two sides of the same coin."[29] This indicates that studies about congregational leadership cannot be isolated from the congregational cultures in which they flourish. Although a community may be considered as a larger culture, this study focuses on the internal cultural dimension. In Browning's language, the larger culture is assumed to form the context, the "environmental-social-level."[30]

DEFINITIONS OF KEY TERMS

It is important to define some key terms before moving ahead. First is *culture*. Culture is a notoriously ambiguous term.[31] Culture within the humanities disciplines enjoys massive academic treatment in reference to popular forms of life incorporated within the range of notions including context, community, convention, and norm.[32] According to Clifford Geertz, far from its popular use (such as "cultured person" or "cultured society"), *culture* "denotes a historically transmitted pattern of meaning embodied in

---

26. Ammerman, *Studying Congregations: A New Handbook.*
27. Callahan, *Religious Leadership,* 38.
28. Dearman, *Religion and Culture in Ancient Israel,* 3.
29. Schein, *Organizational Culture and Leadership,* 1.
30. Browning, *Fundamental Practical Theology,* 71.
31. Phillips, "More Than a Passover," 31.
32. Tanner, *Theories of Culture,* ix.

symbols, a system of inherited conceptions expressed in symbolic forms by means of which human beings communicate, perpetuate and develop their knowledge about, and their attitudes towards life."[33] Perhaps Aylward Shorter's definition best describes what culture is: "a transmitted pattern of meanings embodied in symbols, a pattern capable of development and change, [which] belongs to the concept of humanness itself."[34] If culture is central to what it is to be human, then the hypothesis that religion is a cultural system finds much expression in it.

The concept of culture is significant for this study because the broader framework within which our actions are determined is shaped by the culture in which we are embedded. This implies that cultural factors determine leadership situations. Leadership is exercised and shaped within values of particular cultures. Using Cliffort Geertz's *Interpretation of Culture*, this study will identify congregational cultures (or meaning-making) based on words, actions, gestures, relationships, and so on that are used among members as a way to identify culture's impact on the formation and empowerment of leaders in the EECMY.

The second term is *missional leadership*. The term *missional leadership* merged from the use of two terms (*missional* and *leadership*) which were welded together for the first time when the missional church conversation started in the 1990s. In *Missional Church*, one chapter deals with the missional church conversation and its implications for current leadership practice in the church.[35] According to Roxburgh, the intention of the authors was that "by modifying the noun leadership with the adjective missional there would be a functional reorientation in the life of the churches."[36]

According to Roxburgh, there has been a "wrong turn" in the last few decades in the way missional church language has been used. This "wrong turn" was the use of missional language in relation to the activity of the church as a representative of God to the world, and was made to justify former strategies like church growth, effective church ministry, etc. Roxburgh argues that this approach had its own impact on the way missional leadership was to be understood, and has led a situation in which "missional leadership continues to be framed as some subset of existing forms of

33. Geertz, *Interpretation of Cultures*, 89.

34. Shorter, *Theology of Inculturation*, 5.

35. Guder and Barrett, *Missional Church: A Vision for the Sending of the Church in North America*.

36. Roxburgh, "Missional Leadership," 129.

church leadership."[37] Therefore, he contends that there should be a radical reorientation on the way missional leadership is defined and used. For him, "what God is doing in the world must be the starting point for articulating a missional leadership."[38]

The third term is *spiritual formation*. James Wilhoit defines spiritual formation as "intentional communal process of growing in our relationship with God and becoming conformed to Christ through the power of the Holy Spirit."[39] Christ is the new Adam into whose image we are being formed. Mark Lau Branson and Juan F. Martinez explores four different kinds of formations includes the following: *spiritual formation, congregational formation*, and *missional formation. Spiritual formation* asks what God is up to in the life of a congregation. *Congregational formation* is about "social formation"—how people interact with each other within the congregation. *Missional formation*, on the other hand, is "how God shapes a church to participate in God's love for the world."[40] In short, for Branson and Martinez, "a church's identity and agency are shaped by how we attend to God, to each other and to the world we live in."[41]

SIGNIFICANCE OF THE STUDY

As described in the above sections, this research engages the missional church conversation from an African perspective. This conversation has sought to understand the church's identity related to mission within the rapidly changing, post-Christendom and postmodern world of the United States. Though this conversation has a worldwide significance in terms of creating a scenario for universal conversation regarding the form and identity of the church in our age, it has taken place most vigorously in the American and European contexts.

In this new apostolic age, however, context is a critical dimension of analysis. Attention is rightly paid to worldviews and how identities are determined by social location and other factors. Social and geographical locations are especially critical in determining the kind and form of

---

37. Roxburgh, "Missional Leadership," 129–30.

38. Roxburgh, "Missional Leadership," 130.

39. Wilhoit, *Spiritual Formation*, 23.

40. Branson and Martínez, *Churches, Cultures*, 60–64.

41. Branson and Martínez, *Churches, Cultures*, 61.

missional engagement of a congregation in a given society.[42] This means African Christians' understanding of the missional identity of the church and their practice of leadership formation have some differences from that of westerners. The researcher aims at exploring such praxis as a means to both initiating a missional church conversation in the African context and to contributing to the global conversation on the nature and form of theology from an African perspective.

This study intends to contribute to current theological research by looking carefully at the complexity of congregations in different contexts and revealing the complexity, ambiguity, and paradoxes found in congregational life. A growing amount of research has been published in the last few years which focuses on "congregational studies." Patrick Keifert describes the approach that began to consider congregations as loci of theology as the "return to the congregations."[43] This "return" is related to the consideration of the significance of the study of congregations by sociologists of religion, historians of religion, and biblical scholars as an important *sitz im leben* for theological construction.[44] Congregational studies are therefore an emerging phenomenon.

These studies attempt to address the relationship between congregational life and theology. There are two main concerns of contemporary congregational studies: how theology emerges from within the life of the congregations, and how these emerging congregational theologies develop the prophetic task.[45] These studies unpack the mystery behind the relationship between the church and God, and the relationship between the church and the world, through careful analysis of the experience of these congregants, both personal and communal.[46] One of the contributions of this research for churches in Africa is to start a conversation about the significance of the study of congregational practice for understanding Christian leadership better. This study joins the voice of those who are attempting to show the significance of studying Christian leadership from the congregations' perspective, and how it helps to better understand God's mission from an indigenous perspective. In return, as David Kelsey argues, the

---

42. See Van Gelder, *Missional Church*.

43. Keifert, *Testing the Spirits*, 17.

44. Ammerman, *Studying Congregations*; Bass, *Practicing Congregation*; Noll, *History of Christianity*; Ammerman and Farnsley, *Congregation and Community*.

45. Barrett, *Treasure in Clay Jars*, x–xi; Simpson, *Critical Social Theory*.

46. Keifert, *Testing the Spirits*, 17.

study proposes a way through which theological institutions are enabled to produce fully formed and adequately skilled ministers and leaders for the church.[47] The study also proposes the way congregations are enabled to serve as a primary location where people are formed into "a public identity with Christ."[48]

SUMMARY AND CONCLUSION

In this era of mission, God is inviting the church to "join in this new adventure in the life of God and world, gospel, church, culture."[49] The question is: how are churches responding to this invitation? The study about missional church and missional leadership is a theological exploration that attempt to respond to such a question. The study that follows explores the culture of four Oromo-speaking EECMY congregations that have set sail on this new adventurous journey and how emerging leaders are formed and empowered by those cultures.

Chapter 2 deals with the literature review focusing on the most important research done related to the research topic. Chapter 3 of this thesis presents theological and biblical framework for the research followed by the theoretical framework in chapter 4. Chapter 5 describes the simple exploratory methodology employed in conducting the research in four congregations, including research design, data gathering, and analysis. Chapter 6 provide the result of the study. Chapter 7 presents theological and biblical reflection frameworks of the research mainly engaging the implication of social Trinity for missional church and missional leadership in the EECMY context. This is followed by a theoretical reflection on the research guided by two major theories: theories of culture and leadership theories. The postlude of the chapter will offer a summary and conclusion of the research.

---

47. Kelsey, *Understand God Truly.*
48. Keifert, *Testing the Spirits,* 23.
49. Keifert, *We Are Here Now,* 36–37.

Chapter 2

LITRATURE REVIEW

THIS RESEARCH ENGAGES ITSELF with the question of how the culture of the EECMY congregations engaged in holistic ministry forms and empowers missional leaders. Theologically speaking, two main perspectives inform this research. First, this research is grounded in the theological field of Congregational Studies, because study of the cultures of congregations engaged in holistic ministry requires careful analysis of the social, cultural, and religious aspects of congregational activities. Such study about the identity and ministry of the church (especially with respect to leadership) also demands careful dealings with missional church literature. Second, the particular focus of this research, EECMY congregations, demands a careful review of available resources on Ethiopian Christianity.

CONGREGATIONAL STUDIES AND HOLISTIC MINISTRY

The study of congregations has been an ongoing reality since the beginning of the twentieth century. However, it was in the 1980s that the field of inquiry called "Congregational Studies" emerged.[1] By definition, Congregational Studies focuses on specific individual communities. Most studies have integrated social science methodologies with theological methods to study how congregations perceive themselves, their context, and their

---

1. Keifert, *Testing the Spirits*, 17.

mission.[2] The results of such research have shown that congregations have the capacity to engage in substantive conversations that can illuminate the activity of God in their midst.[3]

Congregation and Community, by Nancy Tatom Ammerman et al., is the "best study of congregations to have appeared in the past seventy years."[4] According to Ammerman and Farnsley, the main purpose of the study is to understand "the role of congregations in the midst of community change."[5] In her book, Ammerman studies nine communities in four different locations in America (the west, southeast, northeast, and midwest), where pairs of churches were chosen with the hope of determining how these church communities had responded to significant changes that had taken place in the community. This research has stimulated other studies about multidimensional ministries of congregations.

In her book, Ammerman identifies six categories under which congregational studies can be conducted.[6] These include the following: ecological studies (the study about the sociology of church and community),[7] cultural studies (focusing on congregation as community),[8] process studies (an analysis of the ways congregations organize themselves),[9] resource studies (dealing with the fiscal resource of congregations),[10] leadership,[11] and theological studies.[12] Her work provides a sociological frame for understanding congregations that are facing significant change in their external environments. How does the nature of such congregations relate to the way they respond to changes occurring in their own context? Ammerman and Farnsley conclude that "the social process of community formation governs

2. Barrett, *Treasure in Clay Jars*, 52.

3. Keifert, *Testing the Spirits*.

4. Stewart, "Emergence of Congregational Studies," 282.

5. Ammerman and Farnsley, *Congregation and Community*, 4.

6. Ammerman and Farnsley, *Congregation and Community*, 346.

7. Dudley, *Civil Investing by Religious Institutions*; Ammerman and Farnsley, *Congregation and Community*; Dudley, *Basic Steps*; Robert Wuthnow, *Loose Connections*.

8. Dudley and Johnson, *Energizing the Congregation*; Nancy Tatom Ammerman, *Bible Believers*.

9. Edgell, *Congregations in Conflict*.

10. Hoge, *Money Matters*; Wuthnow, *Crisis in the Churches*.

11. Carroll, *As One with Authority*; Wimberly, *Recalling Our Own Stories*.

12. Bass, *Practicing Our Faith*; Browning, *Fundamental Practical Theology*.

the rise and fall of congregations; and the spiritual energies generated in congregations help shape the social structure of communities."[13]

For the purpose of this research, my review of the literature will focus on four of the categories identified by Ammerman and Farnsley: ecology, culture, leadership, and theology. The reason for focusing on these four categories is that the interest of this research is mainly focused on identifying the outcomes of the interaction between the ecological, cultural, and theological study of the congregations (particularly the EECMY) and the leadership aspects of the study.

From among congregational studies focusing on the ecological and cultural aspects, the work of Ronald Sider, Philip Olson, and Heidi Unruh represent one prominent resource. This book deals with issues that are related to "the complex but complementary patterns of data on the proportions of offering social services, the congregational characteristics associated with social activism, the range and capacity of the service provided, and the resources and collaborations that make them possible."[14] In their work, they identify fifteen of one hundred and forty-five congregations which they describe as "holistic," and describe how these congregations engage with the wider public.

James Hopewell's *Congregation: Stories and Structures* is also a helpful resource which has had a lasting influence on congregational studies.[15] This book explores how Christian community realizes its identity and understands its mission through common discernment. In this book, Hopewell uses ethnography and literary criticism to construct a new theory of congregations and their culture. Using narratives, congregational "plots," metaphors, and "thick description," he describes congregations as webs of stories. He posited that stories of members of a given congregation are ways through which one can engage the worldviews and value systems of the congregants. His work is a phenomenal resource for understanding how an innovative account of a congregation as a cultural phenomenon allows a collective identity to emerge through the stories congregational members tell about themselves.

A study by Charles Van Engen, *God's Missionary People*, is another book which is helpful for understanding how the inner nature of congregations

13. Ammerman and Farnsley, *Congregation and Community*, 2–3.

14. Sider, Olson, and Unruh, *Churches That Make a Difference*; Unruh, Olson, and Network, "Becoming a Church That Makes a Difference."

15. Hopewell, *Congregation: Stories and Structures*.

as progressive and "consistently becoming," affects the way they engage in mission.[16] This book is aimed at enabling leaders of local congregations to help their members "discover their nature, doing the hard task of setting priorities and goals."[17] Van Engen's work is related to what Nieman James, in his article "Attending Locally," identifies as the seven marks of the church as norms generated by faith communities out of their lived experience.[18]

Testing the Spirits by Patrick Keifert et al., focuses on the theological aspect of congregational study.[19] It illustrates how a careful study about faith-based public moral conversation can happen between and among congregations, and can lead to the production of a relatively adequate theology. The purpose of the study is to support, equip, and encourage the congregations in the effort to learn how to do the work of theology, rather than tell them what they need to know.

Practicing Theology by Miroslav Volf et al., addresses the relationship between the Christian faith (theology) and its practical implications, especially as it emphasizes "the actual lives of Christian individuals, families, and communities" as a place where "theology is [studied as] a communal enterprise."[20] In his other work, *After Our Likeness*, Volf links theological reflection about social Trinity with the nature and mission of a local congregation.[21] In this book, he argues that "in every congregation assembling in Christ's name to profess faith in him, the one and whole Christ is present through his Spirit. For this reason a congregation is not a part of the church but rather the whole church."[22] *Studying Congregations* by Ammerman et al., is another major study that outlines the "state of arts" in contemporary congregational studies.[23] The book is an invitation to systematic theologians and theologians from other disciplines to "engage in a systematic look at congregational life" and to seriously consider individual congregations as centers for theological study.[24] In this study, they contend that when "people of faith, gathered in congregations, work together to make sense of their

16. Van Engen, *God's Missionary People*, 15–18.

17. Van Engen, *God's Missionary People*, 20–21.

18. James, "Attending Locally. Theologies in Congregations."

19. Keifert, *Testing the Spirits*.

20. Volf and Bass, *Practicing Theology*, 5.

21. Volf, *After Our Likeness*.

22. Moltmann, *Church in the Power of the Spirit*, 156.

23. Ammerman, *Studying Congregations*, 9.

24. Ammerman, *Studying Congregations*, 9.

lives and to devise ways of relating to the divine powers that lie within and beyond them," what happens is theological.[25] This book is a revision of the earlier *A Handbook for Congregational Studies*. [26] The emphasis of this book is on providing a framework for an enriched understanding of the nature of the congregations that is centered on four interrelated congregational patterns: identity, context, process, and program.

David Kelsey's *To Understand God Truly* is a book that frames theological conversation between congregations and theological institutions.[27] Kelsey's central argument is that the "emphasis of theological schools should be the understanding of God as well as transforming individuals and communities"[28] through capacitating school leaders and theologians "to understand Christian congregations as diverse concrete of the Christian thing."[29]

When it comes to the leadership aspect of congregational studies, the work of Jackson W. Carroll's *As One with Authority* is an essential study that focuses on reclaiming a healthy understanding of leadership in local congregations. [30] He contends that the understanding of healthy leadership happens by reviewing the meaning of the authority of clergy and examining how this authority has been used.

C. Kirk Hadaway's *Behold I Do a New Thing* is another significant resource because it identifies four types of congregational models.[31] The first is the *club* or *clan*. This type is exemplified by the type of congregational community that exists primarily for the purpose of social identity. The second type is the *charismatic-leader-and-followers model*. The church in this model is a collection of followers rather than a community. The third type is the *church as company or corporation*. In this model, churches tend to become bureaucratic organizations where the true goal is to keep the organization running and the numbers up. The final type is the *incarnational community*. This is the model that Hadaway proposes as the preferred type of congregation. His central argument is that the church should be "a supportive community of faith where people can grow spiritually and learn to

---

25. Ammerman, *Studying Congregations*, 9.

26. Carroll, Dudley, and McKinney, *Handbook for Congregational Studies.*.

27. Kelsey, *Understand God Truly*.

28. Kelsey, *Understand God Truly*.

29. Kelsey, *Understand God Truly*, 250.

30. Carroll, *As One with Authority*.

31. Hadaway, *Behold I Do a New Thing*.

live authentically. The entire system that is the church should support this central purpose—especially its worship services."[32] This, then, leads to the people being transformed. When Hadaway speaks about transformation, he is explicitly referring to the formation and empowerment of leaders— leadership transformation.

Congregational Studies was introduced to Africa through the Network for African Congregational Theology (NetACT), a network of theological institutions in sub-Saharan Africa. These institutions are Presbyterian and Reformed in their tradition, and have not done much to include theological institutions from other denominations. The purpose of this network is "to empower congregations to address their multiple problems, challenges, and sufferings in sub-Saharan."[33] In one of their widely-read publications, *Studying Congregations in Africa*,[34] they outline the need and the how of congregational studies in African context, the how referring to the use of sociological methods of congregational analysis.

MISSIONAL CHURCH AND LEADERSHIP

Missional church literature focuses on identifying the missionary nature of the congregation. These literatures resulted from Leslie Newbigin's critical approach to the encounter between "the gospel and the late-modern western culture."[35] In his book *Foolishness to the Greeks*, Newbigin asks the following question: "What would be involved in a missionary encounter between the gospel and these whole way of perceiving, thinking, and living that we call 'modern western culture'?"[36] As Roxburgh emphasizes, "Newbigin's framing of the missionary situation of the West seemed to offer a fresh and critical window into a new assessment of the church and how its leaders might function."[37]

The Gospel and Our Culture Network contextualized Newbigin's European-based analysis for a North American context. The book *Missional Church*, the second product of this network, concerned itself with the missional character of the church. It identifies the very nature of the church

32. Hadaway, *Behold I Do a New Thing*, 68.

33. Hendriks, *Studying Congregations in Africa*, 11.

34. Hendriks, *Studying Congregations in Africa*, 11.

35. Van Gelder, *Missional Church and Leadership Formation*, 5.

36. Newbigin, *Foolishness to the Greeks*, 1.

37. Roxburgh, "Missional Leadership," 128.

(what the church is and does) in relation to *Missio Dei*.[38] In this book, there is one chapter on church leadership and its implications for missional conversation. David Bosch's seminal work *Transforming Mission* is also another resource with lasting influence on the missional church conversation.[39] One way to read the main arguments in his book is as an account of how "in each historical epoch of the past two millennia the missionary idea has been profoundly influenced by the overall context in which Christians lived and worked."[40] In each of the six epochs that he examines, he provide a meta-perspective on the relationship between the characteristics of church, mission, and missional leadership.

There are very few studies conducted within missional church literature that address missional leadership. A book by Lois Barret et al., *Treasures in Clay Jars*, is one of the few significant contributions to the missional church conversation with a particular emphasis on missional leadership.[41] This book is about the development of missional leaders within a congregational setting. It is a work that signifies a shift from a literature-based approach to a practice-based study of congregations and leadership. According to Barret, this book responds to the criticism she received on an earlier book, *The Missional Church*,[42] whereby critics noted that the contributors did not include practical aspects of congregational life, but were limited to the study of literature.

Eddie Gibbs's *LeadershipNext* studies how newly-established congregations develop missional leadership appropriate to the missional challenges.[43] He underlines that "organizations that are best able to operate within the new cultural reality [in the postmodern era] are flexible, fast-moving and sensitive to the change taking place in their environment."[44] His comprehensive description of the ministry of a missional church as holistic, and his creative work in framing the concept of leadership with Trinitarian theology, is a substantial contribution to the emerging literature on missional leadership.

38. Guder and Barrett, *Missional Church*.

39. Bosch, *Transforming Mission*.

40. Bosch, *Transforming Mission*, 349.

41. Barrett, *Treasure in Clay Jars*.

42. Guder and Barrett, *Missional Church*.

43. Gibbs, *Leadershipnext*.

44. Gibbs, *Leadershipnext*, 97.

Alan Roxburgh and Fred Romanuk's *The Missional Leader* moves the conversation toward the question of how missional theology informs the practice of leadership.[45] Their concept of missional theology centers mainly on "the memory of biblical narratives."[46] The primary task of a leader in missional congregations is to correlate the social context of the members with the memory of the larger narrative in Scripture. They argue that missional leadership is primarily concerned with cultivation of an environment in which members are able to engage in dialogue—dialogue that would lead to locating oneself "within God's narratives."[47]

Scott Cormode's *Making Spiritual Sense* identifies a congregational leader as a "manager of meaning," which means a leader provides a theological framework for action.[48] In his article "Cultivating Missional Leaders," he also offers the concept of the "mental model," whereby he proposes that leadership formation should be viewed from the point of view of "ecology of vocation"—a careful and constructive approach to the "experience persons have had as they come into leadership roles."[49] *Theology of Church Leadership* by Larry Richard and Clyde Hoeldtke's highlights the importance of body theology for understanding church leadership.[50] *The Missional Church and Leadership: Helping Congregations Develop Leadership Capacity* by Craig Van Gelder et al., is another helpful resource that demonstrates how the missional church conversation can be taken as a strategy to help American church es reconfigure their practices for training leaders.[51] Finally, Henri Nouwen's work *In the Name of Jesus* helps to frame what distinctly Christian leadership looks like.[52]

STUDIES ON MISSION AND LEADERSHIP IN ETHIOPIA

Christianity in Ethiopia has been the focus of historical research for decades. Until few decades ago, however, it was the Orthodox Church that has been the object of so many scholarly works. The significant aspect of these

45. Roxburgh and Romanuk, *Missional Leader*.
46. Roxburgh and Romanuk, *Missional Leader*, 69.
47. Roxburgh and Romanuk, *Missional Leader*, 69.
48. Cormode, *Making Spiritual Sense*.
49. Van Gelder, *Missional Church and Leadership Formation*, 97.
50. Richards and Hoeldtke, *Theology of Church Leadership*.
51. Van Gelder, *Missional Church and Leadership Formation*.
52. Nouwen, *Name of Jesus*.

studies is that the role of religion is well-integrated into general studies of the early development of the Ethiopian state and society.

In the study of the history and heritage of evangelical Christianity in Ethiopia, western missionaries are to be credited for their foundational and rigorous works. In particular, Norwegian and Swedish missionaries have immensely contributed to the study of evangelical Christianity in Ethiopia—the EECMY in particular. However, these studies have been criticized for reflecting primarily the missionaries' viewpoints rather than those of the indigenous people. In the last few years, Ethiopian scholars who had the opportunity to study abroad have also been able to contribute their perspective to the resources available on evangelical Christianity in Ethiopia.

About thirty years ago, Paul Jenkins noted that the studies conducted on African religion history and practice were focused on the activities of western missionaries. According to Jenkins, this has resulted in the description of Christian faith and practices as foreign to the local community. Therefore, he contends, the focus has to shift to the question of indigenization—to the study of interaction between cultural tradition and Christian faith.[53]

Prior to the writing of Gustave Arén in 1978, the Ethiopian scholarship was similar to that of all other African countries. There was no major scholarly study on the history, tradition, and cultural expression of evangelical Christians as such. Those resources that were available were books and articles written by missionaries as a report about their work in Ethiopia—the mission field. A major study that gave due consideration to the contribution of the local people was first conducted by Arén in his *Evangelical Pioneers in Ethiopia*.[54] In his book, he acknowledges and meticulously narrates the account of indigenous leaders and ministers. His other work, *Envoys of the Gospel in Ethiopia: In the Steps of the Evangelical Pioneer*, was exploratory research for latter studies about mission, leadership, growth and history of the EECMY.[55] His work can be considered the first study on congregational history of the EECMY because his research was based on the history of the disintegrated Lutheran congregations in Ethiopia before the formation of the confederation of congregations (in the 1940s and 1950s) and before the EECMY was established as a national church in 1959.

53. Jenkins, "Roots of African Church History," 68.

54. Arén, *Evangelical Pioneers in Ethiopia*.

55. Arén, *Envoys of the Gospel in Ethiopia*.

Almost all studies mentioned below have depended to a significant extent on his seminal works.

O. Sæverås's *Church-Mission Relations in Ethiopia 1944–1969* is an interesting text that lays a good foundation for the study of leadership in the early history of the EECMY.[56] It is the story about the early attempt of the Ethiopian church leaders (which were simply congregational leaders) to establish an independent Evangelical Church in 1944, an attempt which finally failed due to the opposition of the missionaries, and how these leaders were able stand against the missionaries divisive ideologies in forming the EECMY in 1959.

Øyvind Eide's seminal work *Revolution and Religion in Ethiopia* describes the dynamics between religion and politics in Ethiopia.[57] Eide's main emphasis is on how the EECMY as a church that emerged from a marginalized community, the "periphery," relates to the institutions and cultures of those in authority at the "center." Basing his research on the Western Synod of the EECMY, the birth-place of Lutheranism in Ethiopia, he undertakes a critical analysis of how the EECMY congregations functioned in the socio-economic, socio-religious, and socio-political landscape of the revolutionary Marxist government of Ethiopia. His notion of center-periphery dynamics of the Ethiopian society helps us understand the context within which the EECMY leaders were being formed and empowered for decades.

Johnny Bakke's published dissertation, *Christian Ministry*, is another important source which provides a good overview of the background of evangelical believers in Ethiopia, particularly the EECMY.[58] In his dissertation, Bakke attempts to describe the identity of the EECMY ministers by carefully analyzing the interplay between Orthodox faith, missionaries' tradition, and traditional religions in Ethiopia. Throughout his work, he attempts to show that leadership roles in the EECMY are shaped by the traditional leadership cultures among the Oromo and Sidama, the two ethnic groups from which the EECMY draws most of its members.

Arne Tolo's *Sidama and Ethiopian* is another dissertation dealing with the establishment of the EECMY church in the southern part of Ethiopia among the people of Sidama.[59] His study focuses on analysis of

56. Sæverås, *Church-Mission Relations in Ethiopia*.

57. Eide, *Revolution and Religion*.

58. Bakke, *Christian Ministry: Patterns and Functions within the Ethiopian Evangelical Church Mekane Yesus*.

59. Tolo, *Sidama and Ethiopian*.

the socio-cultural, socio-political, and the religious tradition of the Sidama people with the purpose of identifying the connecting point between their conditions and the evangelical gospel preached to them by missionaries. He also gives due consideration to study of the impact of evangelical faith on the social, cultural, and political life of the Sidama people.

Johannes Launhardt's book *Evangelicals in Addis Ababa: 1919–1991* is another historical study that provides a detailed account of the foundation and growth of the EECMY synod in and around Addis Ababa—the capital city of Ethiopia.[60] Staffan Grenstedt's book *Ambaricho and Shonkolla: From Local Independent Church to the Evangelical Mainstream in Ethiopia* is another resource that helps us to understand the concept of indigenous leadership in the EECMY context.[61] His study is focused on the analysis of how the Christian community in the Kambata/Hadiya area became independent congregations, and how these congregations were later able to form a union that was later integrated as a synod of the EECMY. Eskil Forslund's *The Word of God in Ethiopian Tongues* is an analytic description of the rhetorical characteristics of the preaching in the EECMY.[62] His study can be described as the first attempt to describe the theology of local congregations based on the rhetorical speech in congregational preaching.

Fekadu Gurmessa's recent study *Evangelical Faith Movement in Ethiopia: Origins and Establishment of the Ethiopian Evangelical Church Mekane Yesus* is a continuation from Arén's work to bring the history of the EECMY to completion.[63] It is a good study that narrates the history of the EECMY beginning with the social, political, and economic environment within which the evangelical movement started in Ethiopia and culminating with the documentation of how the EECMY was established as a national church in 1959. The Amharic edition of this book was first published in 1999. Its wide acceptance and the increasing demand among evangelical believers and seminaries in Ethiopia resulted in the publication of the English version in 2009. Debela Birri's *Divine Plan Unfolding* is a historical work dealing with the emergence, development, and growth of the Evangelical Church Bethel until its merger with its longstanding sister church, the EECMY, in 1974.[64]

60. Launhardt, *Evangelicals in Addis Ababa*.

61. Grenstedt, *Ambaricho and Shonkolla*.

62. Forslund, *Word of God in Ethiopian Tongues*.

63. Gurmessa, *Evangelical Faith Movement in Ethiopia*.

64. Birri, *Divine Plan Unfolding*.

Among the work of scholars from different disciplines, works by Tamerat Taddesse (*Church and State in Ethiopia*), Donald Crummey (*Priests and Politicians: Protestant and Catholic Missions in the Orthodox Ethiopia, 1830–1868*), Bahru Zewde (*A History of Modern Ethiopia 1855–1974*), H.G. Marcus (*The Modern History of Ethiopia*), and John Spencer Trimingham (*The Christian Church and Mission in Ethiopia*) are classics in this field[65] for understanding the relationship between church and state in Ethiopia. However, starting from the time of the socialist government in Ethiopia (1974–1991), these studies have been under critical evaluation by scholars from different disciplines within and outside Ethiopia since they were written from the perspective of imperial Ethiopia, that is, by those at the "center" of the authority who held a negative view of the history, culture, and social structures of the marginalized communities.

From the scholars that emerged from among the people at the periphery, Mohammed Hassan's work *The Oromo of Ethiopia* is a major study that critically analyzes the socio-cultural and socio-political developments in the marginalized communities of Ethiopia.[66] A book by Asafa Jalata, *Contending Nationalisms of Oromia and Ethiopia: Straggle for Statehood, Sovereignty, and Multinational Democracy,* recapitulates the major historical events and proposes the adoption of Oromo democracy as an alternative to the existing exploitive system in Ethiopia.[67]

Among historians, a study by Richard Pankhurst, *The Ethiopian Borderlands: Essays in Regional History from Ancient Times to the End of the 18th Century,* is a major challenge to previous hegemonic studies of the center in that it focuses on the Ethiopian peripheries.[68] The strongest challenge to the former studies on Ethiopian history, culture, and politics comes from the publications of the proceedings of the Oromo Studies Association (OSA), an association with a legacy that spans over twenty-five years.

A publication of Negaso Gidada (the former president of Ethiopia), *The Introduction and Expansion of Orthodox Christianity*, and P.T. W. Baxter's work *Being and Becoming Oromo* are some of the major works that describe and analyze the Oromo perspectives on history, culture, politics

65. Taddesse, *Church and State in Ethiopia*; Crummey, *Priests and Politicians*; Zewde, *History of Modern Ethiopia*; Marcus, *Modern History of Ethiopia*; Trimingham, *Christian Church and Missions in Ethiopia*.

66. Hassen, *Oromo of Ethiopia*.

67. Jalata, *Contending Nationalisms of Oromia and Ethiopia : Struggling for Statehood, Sovereignty, and Multinational Democracy.*

68. Pankhurst and Kane, *Ethiopian Borderlands*.

and religion in Ethiopian context.[69] Lambert Bartels' study *Oromo Religion: Myths and Rights of the Western Oromo of Ethiopia* is one of few studies that attempt to describe the Oromo spirituality apart from Christianity and Islam.[70] Bartel was a practicing Catholic missionary and anthropologist who lived in Dembi Dollo, Wallaga from 1968–1980. With support of the Vincentian fathers, he spent some years studying the Oromo. His study, however, is an academic exploration of the features of Oromo culture which is detached from the experience of the people and the complex interplay of religious traditions.

69. Gidada and Crummey, *Introduction and Expansion of Orthodox Christianity*; Baxter et al., "Being and Becoming Oromo."

70. Bartels, *Oromo Religion*.

Chapter 3

THEOLOGICAL AND BIBLICAL PERSPECTIVES

THE AIM OF THIS study is to explore the culture of leadership formation in the African context. Chapter 2 presented previous studies on missional church, missional leadership, and the history and leadership practices of churches in Ethiopia. This chapter presents the theological and biblical concepts that are helpful to the research question: How do cultures of EECMY congregations engaged in holistic ministry form and empower missional leaders?

In this chapter, the researcher will use two theological concepts, the doctrine of Trinity and missional leadership, to engage the research question. The doctrine of the Trinity is particularly a helpful resource for understanding congregations as communities of believers. This research will mainly focus on perichoretic understandings of the social Trinity as a general theological framework for understanding the church and its leadership. Next, the theological concept of the missional leadership is used as a framework for the study of the missional identity and cultures of the EECMY congregations, and to explore the leadership praxis of the EECMY congregations. In addition, the biblical concept of holistic ministry, church, and leadership is developed from the Gospel of Luke and the book of Acts as a framework.

THEOLOGICAL PERSPECTIVES

The Doctrine of the Trinity

What do we find in the description of the Trinity that is relevant for the way we understand the church and its mission? For centuries, the word "mission" was understood as activities or divine responsibilities carried out by the church for "saving souls." Mission was all about what the church and mission organizations do.[1] It was the focus on the doctrine of the Trinity and its relevance for the church's engagement in our world that reoriented the way mission was understood.[2]

It was Karl Barth who first associated the meaning of mission with the Trinity. As he explains, "the term mission was in the ancient church an expression of the doctrine of the Trinity—namely the expression of the divine sending forth of self, the sending of the Son and Holy Spirit to the World."[3] What is missing here, according to Barth, is the connection between the Trinity and "the gathering, forming, and sending of the church into the world"[4] in obedience to Jesus' command in Matthew 28 to go and make disciples of all nations. This way, he initiated the conversation by pointing to the Trinity, rather than the church, as the starting point in talking about mission.

At the conference organized by the International Missionary Council (IMC) held at Willingen in 1952, Barth's concept of the Trinity as foundation for the mission of the church got support. Johannes Blauw, in his book published in 1962, *The Missionary Nature of the Church,5* formulated and gave full expression to the term *missio Dei*—God's mission. Lesslie Newbigin, as active participant in the Willingen conference and other subsequent conferences organized by the IMC, had the chance to reflect on mission from the Trinitarian perspective. His book published in 1978, *The Open Secret,* is his initial articulation of mission from the perspective of the Triune God.

---

1. Guder and Barrett, *Missional Church*; Bosch, *Transforming Mission*; Van Gelder and Zscheile, *Missional Church in Perspective*.

2. Van Gelder, *Ministry of the Missional Church*, 18; Gary Simpson, "No Trinity, No Mission," 264–71.

3. Thomas, *Classic Texts in Mission*, 106. This quote was from Barth's presentation on Brandenburg Mission Conference in 1932.

4. Van Gelder and Zscheile, *Missional Church in Perspective*, 27.

5. Blauw, *Missionary Nature of the Church*.

There are two interrelated concepts that are foundation in the Trinity. First, the Trinity is best understood as being-in-relation, rather than being in itself. As LaCugna rightly notes, the divine persons are not to be thought of as discrete individuals, but as persons who do not exist except in relationship to each other.[6] In her own words, as she contends, "[t]he doctrine of the Trinity affirms that the essence of God is relational, other-word, that God exists as diverse persons united in the communion of freedom, love, and knowledge."[7] Second, the relationship that exists among the members of the Trinity is also extended to the whole creation in such a way that every being is defined in terms of its relationship with the Triune God, each other as human beings, and the whole of creation. As Bonhoeffer rightly notes, God's revelation is a social reality, a relational encounter.[8]

According to LaCugna, "a relational ontology understands both God and the creature to exist and meet as persons in communion [in such a way that] a relational ontology focuses on personhood, relationship, and communion as the modality of all existence."[9] How we live out interpersonal relationships faithfully as creatures is basically formed and informed by how we perceive the interpersonal relationships of the Trinity. As Crosby notes, "the relationship that exists among members of the Trinity provide powerful insight into how God wants us to relate to one another in community."[10] Equally, our personhood as human beings both informs and is informed by our perception of the personhood of the Father, the Son, and the Holy Spirit. It delineates the way in which we as Christians are invited to participate in the divine life on a daily basis.[11]

As LaCugna noted, it is this "proper subject matter of the doctrine of the Trinity" that helps us define the framework through which the church relates to God and the community it serves—which is "the encounter between divine and human persons in the economy of redemption."[12] The doctrine of Trinity depicts God as the one who is able to identify himself with ordinary people, sharing their daily struggle for life. It is also foundational to seeing mission as part and parcel of God's identity. As Simpson

6. Newbigin, *Open Secret*, 246.

7. LaCugna, *God for Us*, 243.

8. Green, *Bonhoeffer*, 2.

9. LaCugna, *God for Us*, 243.

10. Crosby, *Teaming Church: Ministry in the Age of Collaboration*, 138.

11. LaCugna, *God for Us*, 400.

12. LaCugna, *God for Us*, 305.

also describes, it provides the apostolic difference needed by congregations in such a way that it can reverse the present "abated apostolicity" of the church.[13]

The doctrine of Trinity takes as its grounding theme the perichoretic imagination for the life of the Trinitarian God. *Perichoresis* is a word used to describe the social aspect of Trinity—the intimate indwelling of the three persons without mixing or separation and its implication to the way God relates to the world. According to LaCugna, the concept of perichoresis is used to express the idea that "the three divine persons mutually inhere in one another, draw life from one another, 'are' what they are by relation to one another. Perichoresis means being-in-one-another, permeation without confusion."[14] As Moltmann also explains, "all relationships which are analogues to God reflects the primal, reciprocal indwelling and mutual interpenetration of the Trinitarian Perichoresis."[15]

Perichoresis is not only the very essence of the Triune God's unity, it is also the means by which the Triune God engages the world—the *perichoresis of creation*.[16] As Moltmann contends, the whole of creation is embraced by the Trinity and invited into the eternal divine shared communion because the "perichoretic unity of the divine persons is so wide open that the whole world can find room and rest and eternal life within it."[17] In other words, Perichoresis is about "God in the world and the world in God; heaven and earth in the kingdom of God, pervaded by his glory; soul and body united in the life-giving Spirit to a human whole; women and man in the kingdom of unconditional and unconditional love."[18] Therefore, as Moltmann notes, the term *perichoresis* denotes the fact that "salvation of the creatures exists in their being included in the eternal life of the Triune God and in participating in it."[19]

Perichoresis is a significant term used to frame the identity of church and its mission. As Volf rightly indicates, the analogy of *perichoresis* is basic for the way we understand the relationship between the Triune God and the church (and through the church to the world) because "the Trinity indwells

---

13. Simpson, "No Trinity, No Mission."

14. LaCugna, *God for Us*, 271.

15. Moltmann, *God in Creation*, 17.

16. Cunningham, *Three Are One*, 180.

17. Moltmann, "Perichoresis," 117.

18. Moltmann, *God in Creation*, 17.

19. Moltmann, "Perichoresis," 117.

in the local churches in no other way than through its presence within the persons constituting those churches, since the church is those who gather in the name of Christ."[20] As Moltmann also notes,

> The community of disciples of Christ not only "corresponds" by analogy to the divine Trinitarian community, but also is to become a community in the divine community of the Triune God so that "they [may] also be in us" (John 17:21). This is the mystical dimension of the church.[21]

Some theologians make the mistake of describing the Trinity as an ideal model that congregations are supposed to adopt in their life and ministry. Robert Crosby, for example, argues that "the Trinity is the premier *model*, or the master image, of what Christian fellowship, community, and teamwork are to look like for the purpose of edification, evangelization, and ultimately, the glorification of God on earth."[22] Such an approach promotes the assumption that the Trinitarian doctrine is simply a "model" to be adopted in congregational settings. This, on the other hand, results in a situation where the Trinitarian doctrine might be understood as a law (or principle or idea) that congregations are supposed to live up to in church and society. Such an understanding to Trinity as model provides an impossible goal that, finally, leads to despair.

According to Van Gelder and Zscheile, however, the purpose of the missional church conversation is not to discover a new model or a strategy for church life and ministry, but to provide theological orientation emphasizing the church as an expression of the mission of God.[23] As Alan Hirsch also states, missional church is a theological concept that frames "the role of human agency within the divine agency of the Triune God"[24] by reframing the theology of (about) the church in terms of the mission of God.[25]

However, beyond its significance for providing theological orientation, how do missional church conversations provide us with an understanding of how the church might live out the social implication of the perichoretic

20. Volf, *After Our Likeness*, 203.

21. Moltmann, *Trinity and the Kingdon*, 212.

22. Crosby, *Teaming Church*, 137. Thomas Scirghi also wrongly argues that "the Trinity provides a model for belonging to a community, specially a community of the church." See Scirghi, "Trinity: A Model for Belonging in Contemporary Society," 333.

23. Van Gelder and Zscheile, *Missional Church in Perspective*, 8.

24. Van Gelder and Zscheile, *Missional Church in Perspective*, xviii.

25. Hirsch, "Defining Missional," 22.

life of the Triune God in real life? For this question, the Lutheran under-standing of the church has a meaningful response. The Lutheran under-standing of the church, particularly the Eucharist, is helpful to understand both how the perichoretic life of the Triune God is shared with creation and its implication for the life and ministry of the church.

For this study, which is about how emerging leaders are formed and empowered by cultures of congregations engaged in holistic ministry, the doctrine of the Trinity is taken as a foundational theological framework for understanding the mission and the nature of congregations. It is used to engage the life and ministry of the EECMY congregations involved in ho-listic ministry. The doctrine of the Trinity is significant for understanding the nature of the church and its mission because it is inherently practical, and oriented towards the lived experience of human beings.[26] As LaCugna righty states, it is "ultimately a practical doctrine with radical consequence for Christian life."[27]

The Doctrine of Trinity and Missional Church Conversation

Central to missional church conversation is the notion that mission is de-fined and described from a Trinitarian perspective. The doctrine of Trinity helps us understand what God is up to in the world, and has several impli-cations for what it means to the church that bears witness to the Trinity's passionate presence in this world. In other words, as Guder and Barrett rightly indicates, our understanding about the church and its ministry is shaped by the character and purpose of God. In other words, as they argue, the "Trinitarian point of entry into our theology of the church necessarily shifts all the assents in our ecclesiology."[28]

According to Miroslav Volf, the basic need to connect the doctrine of the Trinity with that of the ministry of the church is to describe "a vision of the church as an image of the Triune God,"[29] to the inner nature of the church. The doctrine of the Trinity helps us understand what it means to engage in God's mission, embody and disclose the love of Christ as a com-munity of believers.[30] As members of the church, Christians are created

26. LaCugna, God for Us.
27. LaCugna, God for Us, 377.
28. Guder and Barrett, Missional Church, 5.
29. Volf, After Our Likeness, 2.
30. Volf, After Our Likeness, 7.

and called to mirror God's image to the world—which implies that the Christian community, in its Trinitarian image, should live in a way that reflects life with the Triune God.[31] This is the very reason why the doctrine of the Trinity is at the heart of the missional church conversation. The essence of missional theology is a particular view of mission as part of God's identity.[32]

According to Bosch, "to say that church is missionary does not mean that mission is church-centered. It is *Missio Dei.* It is Trinitarian."[33] As he contends, "mission [is] understood as being derived from the very nature of God. It [is] thus put in the context of the doctrine of the doctrine of the Trinity, not of ecclesiology or soteriology."[34] Missional ecclesiology that is based on Trinitarian theology reminds us that the church is a sent community—just as the Father sent his Son to the world, and the Father and the Son sent the Spirit, the church is a community of the sent community. As a community of believers, we are all called to be sent to participate fully in God's mission within the whole of creation. As Os Guinness states, God's calling "is personal but not purely individual; Jesus summons his followers not only on an individual calling but also to a corporate calling."[35]

Such understanding about the missional church is used in this research as a theological framework used to explore how cultures of the EECMY congregations engaged in holistic ministry form and empower missional leaders. The missional church concept is used to frame congregational ministries of the EECMY. However, how we apply the missional church concept in studying congregations need some more practical discussion here. For that, Luther's understanding of the church provides us with a good theological framework.

The church, for Luther, is the assembly of all believers among whom the Gospel is proclaimed and sacraments are properly administered.[36] The assembly of all believers is described in the Apostles Creed as *communio sanctorum*, the "communion of saints." Luther's account of the Eucharist (explained below) provides us with a comprehensive view of this communion and its practical expression.

31. Zizioulas and McPartlan, *Communion and Otherness*, 4–5.

32. Guder and Barrett, *Missional Church*, 5.

33. Bosch, *Transforming Mission*, 493.

34. Bosch, *Transforming Mission*, 390.

35. Guinness, *Call*, 70, 78.

36. Augsburg Confession, Article VII.

According to Luther, the Gospel is what leads to the "communion of saints." Luther's argument about the significance of the gospel is similar to Scot McKnight's definition of the gospel. The gospel mediates the Holly Spirit, who "calls, gathers, enlightens, and sanctifies the whole Christian church on earth and preserves it in union with Jesus Christ in the one true faith."[37] In other words, it is the gospel mediated by the Spirit that opens the way for us to share the life of the Triune God by virtue of which we are also enabled to commune with each other. Luther's argument about the significance of the gospel is similar to Scot McKnight's definition of the gospel: "the Gospel is the work of God to restore humans to union with God and communion with others, in the context of a community for the good of others and the world."[38] It is within this definition of the church that we find a more comprehensive and practical explanation of what it means to be a missional church.

According to Luther, "the significance or effect of sacrament is fellowship of all the saints."[39] To take part in Holy Communion is to have fellowship with Christ and all the saints. In the Eucharist, the Triune God shares his Godself with us through bread and wine, and "we become united with Christ, and are made one body with all the saints."[40] As Luther contends, while partaking in the "Blessed Sacrament of the Holy and True Body and Blood of Christ, all the spiritual possessions of Christ and his saints are shared with and become the common property of him who receives this sacraments."[41] Furthermore, According to Luther, in Eucharistic fellowship, "we are [also] to be united with our neighbors, we in them and they in us."[42]

Quoting Luther,

> To receive this sacraments in bread and wine, then, is nothing else than to receive a sure sign of this fellowship and incorporation with Christ and all saints. It is as if a citizen were given a sign, a document, or some other token to assure him [her] that he [she] is a citizen of the city, a member of that particular community.[43]

---

37. Gritsch and Jenson, *Lutheranism*, 124. *Small Catechism*, II, 6.

38. McKnight, *Embracing Grace*, 12.

39. Luther, *Blessed Sacrament*, 50.

40. Luther, *Blessed Sacrament*, 59.

41. Luther, *Blessed Sacrament*, 51.

42. Luther, *Blessed Sacrament,* 51.

43. Luther, *Blessed Sacrament*, 51.

For Luther, there exist a connection between Eucharist and the life and ministry of the church. When we participate in Holy Communion, we take part in "his life and good works, which are indicated by his flesh."[44] To participate in Holy Communion means to share the life of the Triune God (his abundant love and blessing) with the whole of creation—which is manifested through our involvement in the ongoing creative work of God. In taking the blood under the wine, we also take part in "his passion and martyrdom, which are indicated by his blood."[45] We take part in the suffering of Christ that was meant for our salvation, and in the suffering of the whole creation.

In Eucharistic fellowship, all profits and costs are shared. In other words, as joy, support, protection and so on are shared (between God, humanity, and the whole of creation), suffering is also shared within such fellowship. As God partakes in the joys and suffering of creation, the believing community does the same.[46] In Luther's own words, "in this sacrament, man is given through the priest a sure sign from God himself that he is thus united with Christ and his saints and has all things in common [with them], that Christ's suffering and life are his own, together with the lives and sufferings of all the saints."[47]

Additionally, as Luther explains, the Eucharist is the way God offers God's self to the whole of creation, and the believing community responds with thanksgiving. The thanksgiving offered to God is oneself "and all that we have, with constant prayer. With this, we are to yield ourselves to the will of God, that he may make of us what he will, according to his own pleasure."[48]

As described above, Luther's description of the Eucharist provides us with a practical theological framework for understanding how the missional church takes part in the life and in the ongoing creative work of the Triune God. The mission for which the church exists is to partake in the shared life of the Triune God and in the divine reality of being community.

44. Luther, *Blessed Sacrament*, 60.

45. Luther, *Blessed Sacrament*, 60.

46. Luther, *Blessed Sacrament*, 51–52.

47. Luther, *Blessed Sacrament*, 51–52.

48. Luther, *Treatise on the New Testament*, 98.

Missional Leadership

Missional leadership is a theological concept that emerged from the under-standing that leadership should be viewed from a Trinitarian perspective, a perspective that focuses on the ongoing involvement of the Triune God in human history. As Roxburgh rightly articulates, "missional leadership is framed, understood, and articulated in relationship to the question of what God is doing in the world."[49] The starting point in framing missional leadership is a theological reading of God's ongoing creative work.

The research question addressed in this study is how emerging leaders are formed and empowered by cultures of congregations engaged in holis-tic ministry. This question is asked with an understanding that the Triune God is at the center of the formation and empowerment process of the life and ministry of emerging leaders. The social doctrine of the Trinity, particularly the concept of perichoresis, is used as the framework to explore and describe both missional leadership and the cultures of congregations that impact the life of emerging missional leaders.

The concept of Trinity is a useful theological framework to capture missional leadership because it connects the *perichoretic* understanding of the Trinity with the very reason for which the church exists (God's mis-sion) and with the kind of leadership that the church has to exercise for this mission to manifest. As Roxburgh and Romanuk contend, issues related to leadership formation and empowerment should "only [be addressed] in terms of what God is doing in forming the social community known as ecclesia."[50] Understanding missional leadership or how emerging leaders are formed and empowered into becoming missional leaders requires a theological framing of God's work in our world.

As Robert Doornenbal contends, missional leadership is about cul-tural and spiritual formations that happen in the context where "individual participants, groups, and the community as a whole *respond to challeng-ing situations and engage in transformative changes* that are necessary to become, or remain, oriented to God's mission in the local context."[51] Ac-cording to this research, missional leadership is described in conjunction with cultural and spiritual formation (the Triune God being at the center

---

49. Roxburgh, "Missional Leadership," 130; Gibbs, *Leadershipnext*, 38.

50. Roxburgh and Romanuk, *Missional Leader*, 118.

51. Doornenbal, *Crossroads*, 200. Emphasis mine.

of the process) in the context where EECMY congregations are engaged in holistic ministry.

By cultural formation, Doornenbal refers to the dynamic process of formation of (internal) congregational cultures when "acting on cultures, primarily by shaping conversations, including the content of announcements, testimonies, lessons, and sermons" from the perspective of God's mission.[52] Missional leaders form and are also formed by congregational cultures through the process of interacting with their internal as well as external cultures (which is the larger context in which the congregations find themselves). Spiritual formation is the formation of individual members as they continually respond to "the work of the Holy Spirit, in the community of faith, for the sake of the world."[53] Activities of a given congregation, such as communal worship, pastoral counseling, community services, and so on, contribute to spiritual formation. In this study, both cultural and spiritual formations (with an understanding that social Trinity is integral part of both kinds of formations) are considered as significant aspects of the theological framework used to understand the research question.

If missional leadership is about formation of internal cultures while engaging in the ongoing creating work of the Triune God, how can this be expressed in practical terms in such a way that it reflects the life and ministry of the church and those involved in ministry? Such cultural formation takes place in Eucharist fellowship. In the Eucharist, the Triune God shares its entire perichoretic life with the Christian community and the whole creation, and the Christian community is formed and transformed as a result. As Luther explains, in the Eucharist, "Christ has given his holy body for this purpose, that the things signified by the sacrament—the fellowship, the change wrought by love—may be put into practice."[54]

Eucharistic fellowship is a fellowship that requires willingness to share others' burdens and suffering. It is through the practice of such sharing that the Christian community is transformed, and missional leaders emerge. We encounter God in and through each other's life. By carrying each other's burden with the love of Christ, we form a communal culture through which each member is formed into the likeness of Christ. As Luther emphasizes, "by the means of this sacrament, all self-seeking love is rooted out and gives

---

52. Doornenbal, *Crossroads*, 208.

53. Doornenbal, *Crossroads*, 211. Greenman, "Spiritual Formation in Theological Perspective," 24.

54. Luther, *The Blessed Sacrament*, 60.

place to that which seeks the common good of all; and through the change wrought by love there is one bread, one drink, one body, one community."[55] For Luther, to experience such transformation, one must

> Take to heart the infirmities and needs of others, as if they were [one's] own. Then offer to others [his/her] strength, as if it were their own, just as Christ does for [him/her] in the sacraments. This is what it means to be changed into one another through love. . . . To lose one's own form and take on that which is common to all.[56]

Understanding missional leadership from the perspective of the Eucharistic fellowship leads to the recognition of every believer as a leader, agent of formation and empowerment. Eucharistic fellowship is an invitation to a shared leadership. It corresponds to the argument of Cladis that leadership in the missional church is exercised in a relationship (a team-based community).[57] When leadership is exercised in a relationship, everyone in the Christian community becomes a *de facto* leader, which means that they all have a part to play by sharing each other's suffering and forming each other into the likeness of Christ.[58]

Missional leadership as cultural formation is not limited to the church context. It goes beyond that and includes the spheres in which the church, as participant in the Triune God's ongoing creative work, is engaged. This, according to Simpson, includes the civil society in which the missional church

> exhibits a compassionate commitment to other institutions and their predicaments [which] in turn, yields a critical and self-critical—and thus fully communicative—procedure and practice of public engagement; finally, the emerging missional church, as public companion, participates with civil society to create and strengthen the fabric that fashion a life-giving and a life-accountable world.[59]

55. Luther, *The Blessed Sacrament*, 67.

56. Luther, *The Blessed Sacrament*, 61–62.

57. Cladis, *Leading the Team-Based Church*, 10.

58. Gunton, *Promise of Trinitarian Theology*, 26.

59. Simpson, "Reformation Is a Terrible Thing to Waste," 93.

BIBLICAL PERSPECTIVES

Mission and Leadership in the Gospel of Luke and the Book of Acts

The biblical framework used in this research is drawn from the two writings of Luke: the Gospel of Luke and the book of Acts. In the two books that he wrote, Luke provides us with a narrative about the emergence of the church around the Mediterranean world, starting with the life and ministry of Jesus. His major themes are the presence and ministry of the Holy Spirit, the significance of repentance and forgiveness in people's lives, love of neighbors and enemies, and justice in interhuman relationships.[60] The gospel of Luke and the book of Acts are significant for this research because they provide us with foundational insights for the present-day characteristics for the church engaged in holistic ministry and forms of leadership.[61]

Holistic Ministry

The concept of holistic ministry has been used extensively to describe the public ministry of the church.[62] Texts such as Matthew 28:19–20 ("Go, make disciples of all nations") have been used extensively for this purpose. Others have tried to use the term in relation to development in a way that includes the whole community. They describe it as an integrative approach which is based on the economic and social aspect of community development. To some, it refers to the service rendered to the whole person—mind, spirit, and soul.[63]

However, a closer look at the biblical view of holistic ministry, particularly in the gospel of Luke and the book of Acts, reveals that it refers to "a wholehearted embrace and integration of both evangelism and social ministry so that people experience spiritual renewal, socioeconomic uplift, and transformation of their social context."[64] This understanding of holistic ministry emanates from the interpretation of Jesus' prophetic ministry as

60. Bosch, *Transforming Mission*, 87.

61. Sercombe, "Luke's Vision for the Church," 45.

62. DeGlaisse-Walford, *Mission as Holistic Ministry*, 57.

63. Yamamori, "Serving with the Poor in Africa," 124.

64. Sider and Unruh, *Churches That Make a Difference*, 17; Gallagher and Hertig, *Mission in Acts*, 37–44. Bryant Myers also describe it as "one in which compassion, social transformation, and proclamation are inseparably related." Yamamori, Myers, and Conner, *Serving with the Poor in Asia*, 1.

demonstrated in the Gospel of Luke, with its narrative about the Messiah, who, by the power of the Holy Spirit, has come to this world to restore his people (Luke 4:16–21). This restoration is to be manifested in the lives of the poor and the oppressed as compassion and justice prevail. Jesus' messianic role is to be identified in his work of liberation and his prophetic call for justice.[65] This text is then to be used as a framework through which we understand Jesus' healing ministry, the miracles he performed, and his teaching.

The text in Luke 4:16–21 is taken as the basis of the entire gospel of Luke, and can also serve as a prelude to Acts.[66] The text is quoted from Isaiah 61:1. It was God's message to the Israelites shortly after the Babylonian exile, who were "grieving for Zion" (verse 3) because of the destruction of their land. It was a promise from God through his prophet that their present situation would be reversed. Through announcing the year of Jubilee, "the year of the Lord's favor," God showed his concern (which was also encouragement and hope) for the marginalized and the downtrodden community. The phrase "to let the oppressed go free" was taken from Isaiah 58:6. According to Bosch, the word "oppressed" in the text refers to those "who were economically ruined, those who had become bonded slaves and had no hope of ever again escaping from the throttling grip of poverty."[67]

According to Bosch, in the recent biblical academic study, this particular text in Luke has replaced, for all practical purposes, Matthew's "Great Commission," particularly in conciliar and liberation theology circles, "as a key text not only for understanding Christ's own mission but also that of the church."[68] This is mainly because it highlights Jesus, as anointed Messiah, as a good example of the true form and characteristic of Christianity and its practical expression. A focus on Luke 4:16–21 rather than the Matthew 28 diverts our understanding of mission from solely evangelism (the Matthew text) to a holistic approach, yet gives more attention to the involvement of the Triune God in our world.

In the book of Acts, the disciples' life and ministry is described as a continuation of this liberating ministry of Jesus Christ—which is holistic. Their life was a reflection of the Trinity's practice of self-giving.[69]

65. Sider, Olson, and Unruh, *Churches That Make a Difference*, 116.

66. Bosch, *Transforming Mission*, 113.

67. Bosch, *Transforming Mission*, 102.

68. Bosch, *Transforming Mission*, 84.

69. Crosby, *Teaming Church*, 137.

Holistic ministry in Acts is three-dimensional: evangelistic, fellowship (communion), and prophetic. How these three dimensions of ministry are displayed, and how leaders are formed and empowered within the context where congregations are fully engaged in these types of ministries is of particular interest to this research.

The evangelistic aspect of the church's ministry is vividly expressed in Acts, where the disciples are described as those committed to *teaching and preaching*— "preaching the word of God" (Acts 6:2) and "the ministry of the word and sacrament" (Acts 6:4). In Acts, Luke gives emphasis to the actual story of the lives of the apostles focused on teaching in the ongoing life of the Christian community. In Ephesians, Paul continually taught for two years (Acts 19:8). Apollos, after being instructed by Priscilla and Aquilla, was also engaged in teaching the word of God (Acts 18:24–28). These and other similar stories about the commitment of the apostles to teach and instruct the church show the intention of Luke to illustrate to his readers that this particular characteristic of the church is needed for the nourishment and guidance of the believing community.

The social ministry of the church is described in Acts within the *fellowship and communion* shared among believers. One of the areas on which Luke focused while describing the life and ministry of the apostles in the book of Acts is that they devoted themselves to fellowship, the breaking of bread, and helping the needy (Acts 2:42; 4:32). They had "everything in common" to the extent that they were "one soul" (Acts 2:44; 4:32).[70]

This expression of fellowship in Acts is reinforced by the observation that the communal life of believers carries on the pattern of Jesus' fellowship with his disciples, "sinners," and social outcasts. In the Gospel of Luke, this fellowship is expressed in relation to the coming of the Kingdom of God—in that the kind of fellowship Jesus and his disciples share with others is an expression of the anticipation of the fellowship of the new age.[71]

One component of the study in missional ecclesiology is how congregations interact with each other and the community at large. This interaction calls for an engagement in moral vocation—which requires the congregations to exercise their unique identity as "public moral companions."[72] The

70. For more reading on this particular aspect of the ministry of the church, refer to Bartlett, *Ministry in the New Testament*, 134.

71. See Jesus' parable in Luke 16:9. Jesus' last meal with his disciples can also be considered as the celebration of the new age—where the "sinners" and the social outcasts are welcomed into the fellowship of God (Luke 5:33–39; 15:1–32).

72. Simpson, "God, Civil Society, and Congregations as Public Moral Companions,"

communal life of the church involves mutual care, loving accountability, and hospitality.

The socioeconomic and transformational ministry of the church, which others describe as the *prophetic role* the church plays among the community it serves, is demonstrated in the life and ministry of the apostles of Jesus Christ—in that the mission for which they are being commissioned is the same as that attributed to Jesus: healing the sick, casting out demons, and preaching the kingdom of God (Luke 4:43; 8:1; 9:11; 11:20).

In the study of the missional church, one area of focus has been how the congregations can be theologically equipped to live up to their prophetic task—how they can maintain their true biblical image as a prophetic congregation. According to Gary Simpson's argument in *Critical Social Theory*, theology should be done in a way that congregations are enabled to step into their role as prophetic companions in the public sphere.[73]

Luke on Missional Leadership

As described by Alan Raxburgh, missional leadership is "framed, understood, and articulated in relationship to the question of what God is doing in the world."[74] This implies that when defining or articulating missional leadership from a biblical perspective, our fundamental frame of reference should be how God's mission was expressed through the life of Jesus Christ, his disciples, and the church. This should be done in relation to a theological interpretation of what God is up to in our world in our present context.

According to Roxburgh, "the purpose of leadership is to form and equip people."[75] It is mainly about how emerging leaders are formed and equipped through shared life and embody the purpose and direction of the Triune God through Jesus Christ. Such leadership is described as transformational leadership, and is demonstrated in the life and ministry of Jesus Christ and in the post-Pentecost community. The gospel of Luke demonstrates how Jesus impacted and equipped his disciples. In the book of Acts, Luke provides us with a living example on how leaders (the disciples) form and empower missional communities to be demonstrations of God's reign in the midst of the world.

in *Testing the Spirits*, 88.

73. Simpson, *Critical Social Theory*.

74. Roxburgh, "Missional Leadership," 130.

75. Roxburgh, "Missional Leadership: Equipping God's People for Mission," 183.

The best example for missional leadership is the life and ministry of Jesus Christ in relation to his Father and the Holy Spirit. Luke 4:16–21, in particular, describes Jesus' ministry, which is foundational for understanding the characteristics of the church (as described in the above section) and church leadership from a biblical perspective. Jesus' central message for bringing fundamental social, economic, and political change in society provides us with a biblical framework for understanding God's mission and missional leadership as identified in the Scriptures.[76]

There are two fundamental lessons we draw from the above text in Luke relevant for our discussion on leadership from a biblical perspective. First, the text indicates that Jesus' ministry and leadership is characterized by his involvement in the public life of the community. He challenged the norms of the social context of his time. As Walter Brueggeman emphasizes, by announcing the coming of the new age and showing compassion to the poor and the marginalized, Jesus ministered as someone who could provide an alternative hope to the community he served.[77] This indicates that Jesus' leadership can be characterized as prophetic. He was also prophetic in that he interpreted his context in light of the Scripture so that his followers might understand the situation. As Roxburgh states, the major task of missional leaders (as we learn from the ministry of Jesus) is to "understand their context and interpret that context to the church so that a faithful and relevant witness emerges."[78] Second, the text is an indication that Jesus' leadership is holistic in nature. His influence on those who followed him was multi-dimensional. He evoked radical change in spiritual, social, economic, and political practices.

Furthermore, central to the ministry of Jesus, according to Gibbs, is his election of the twelve disciples and the kind of leadership model he showed in his relationship with them. Teaching by example, both in words and deeds, is applied in his entire ministry as a teacher-leader (Luke 24:19). His disciples could learn from him by listening to his teaching, observing the way he interacted with people without any distinction, and working under their master's supervision.[79]

---

76. There are several leadership themes unfolding in Luke's Gospel. The case of Luke 22:24–30 is a periscope that has attracted many scholars. See Nelson, *Leadership and Discipleship*.

77. Brueggemann, *Prophetic Imagination*.

78. Roxburgh, "Missional Leadership," 189.

79. Gibbs, *Leadershipnext*, 117.

In the book of Acts, we find the expression of Jesus' teaching in the life and leadership ministry of the disciples. Acts begin with a story about how the twelve apostles of Jesus had a change of status "from being followers to becoming the leaders of a Christian community."[80] This story is followed by how other leaders also emerged within the Christian community that was engaged in holistic ministry—where mutual care and companionship was at the center of their ministry.

From the life of the disciples, we learn that leadership is a call to both engage our context with the Gospel and lead the community to being formed into the likeness of Jesus Christ. The formation of missional community is the outcome of the focus of disciples in the power of the word of God in changing peoples' life and their commitment to following the leadership of the Spirit. As Roxburgh describes, a lesson we learn from the ministry of the disciples is that "leadership is a calling that both engages the context with the gospel and leads in the formation of a disciplined community."[81]

Both in the gospel of Luke and the book of Acts, the Holy Spirit is prominent in accomplishing God's mission, which was the declaration of the message of repentance and forgiveness intended for "all nations." The Holy Spirit is active in the life and ministry of Jesus and the disciples. As Roxburgh indicates, missional leadership is "rooted in the Spirit's formation of the Post-Pentecost community."[82]

A disciple's form of leadership, as described in Acts, is characterized by a corporate growth in Christ, a growth that does not occur in an isolated setting. According to Lawrence O. Richards et al., growth in the New Testament is described both numerically (Acts 7:7) and "also of maturity and consolation of the community in Christ from which good works naturally grow."[83] The emergence of the disciples and others appointed as leaders happened within the communal setting, where mutual care and responsibility was exercised. Each member of the community participated in the leadership, for everyone had the gift of the Spirit, but leadership was one of the gifts of the Spirit (Rom. 12:8). It is this communal practice of discipleship that is integral to the believing communities' participation in God's

80. Estrada, *Followers to Leaders*, x.
81. Roxburgh, "Missional Leadership," 212.
82. Roxburgh, "Missional Leadership," 184.
83. Hoeldtke, *Theology of Church Leadership*, 45.

mission. It is within this relational context of common experience of faith that growth takes place.

This corporal growth, which is foundational in understanding the biblical concept of the formation and empowerment of leaders, will be used in this research as a biblical framework for understanding missional leadership. Leadership is about the ability to inspire and empower each other as a community of believers by sharing each other's burden in fellowship. It is an authentic opportunity to be part of the perichoretic life of the Triune God expressed in our shared life, and how we make an impact on the lives of others.

According to the New Testament, a congregation is not simply about the gathering of believing community once or twice a week. A congregation is "a federation of teams" that lives in a committed relationship; mission is described in terms of relationship (since it is Trinitarian). A congregation is a group of people that live out their lives for each other and for those that are outside their circle.

SUMMARY AND CONCLUSION

In this chapter, I have described two theological perspectives in addition to biblical perspectives (on holistic ministry and leadership) that are useful to explore the research question. The theological perspectives are the doctrine of the Trinity and missional leadership. The social notion of the Trinity is used to explore the church's participation in God's mission in the world, and how the missional church needs to address its structure and leadership in relation to the Trinity. The focus has been on the significance of the perichoretic relationship of persons in the Trinity for understanding the characteristics of churches and missional leadership. This theological concept also helps us understand the place of God in the formation and empowerment of missional leaders.

The biblical perspectives have been from the gospel of Luke and the book of Acts. An emphasis has been placed on Luke 4:16–21, a helpful text for understanding the multi-dimensional (holistic) ministry of Jesus and how that shaped the life and ministry of disciples as shown in the book of Acts. On the other hand, the book of Acts is used for defining and identifying holistic ministry and leadership from biblical perspective. The life, teaching, and ministry of Jesus in the gospel of Luke, and the ministry and leadership of the disciples (and the church) as the continuation of the unfolding of Jesus's ministry in the book of Acts, have been explored to lay a framework for understanding congregational life and leadership from biblical perspectives.

The next chapter describes the theoretical frameworks that are helpful for understanding the main emphasis of this research, which is to ex¬plore how emerging leaders are formed and empowered by the cultures of EEC-MY congregations engaged in holistic ministry. Besides theological and biblical frameworks provided in this chapter, the social scientific perspectives on culture and leadership are described in the next chapter to explore the research question.

Chapter 4

THEORETICAL PERSPECTIVES

THE PREVIOUS CHAPTER WAS on theological and biblical perspectives that are helpful for exploring the research question. Two theological concepts (social Trinity and missional leadership) were described as theological frameworks helpful to understand and explore the research question. In addition, biblical perspectives on holistic ministry and leadership from the gospel of Luke and the book of Acts were described as biblical frameworks.

In this chapter, two theoretical perspectives are provided to explore the research question, which are: theory of culture and theory of leadership. The concept of culture is helpful for exploring the characteristic of congregations from their own perspective. It also helps to understand the context of the EECMY congregations, and the dynamism that has direct and indirect implications for formation and empowerment of emerging missional leaders. The theory on leadership, on the other hand, is significant for framing factors that re¬sult in the formation and empowerment of missional leaders. It helps to understand how the con¬gregations have developed a leadership culture through which they are enabled to transform the lives of multitudes and become a context in which missional leaders are formed.

Theory of culture is helpful for defining and exploring the culture of the EECMY congregations from their own perspectives. This theory also helps to understand the context of the EECMY congregations, and the dynamism that has direct and indirect implications for formation and empowerment of emerging missional leaders. It helps to understand how the congregations, with members with such experience, have developed a culture through which they are enabled to transform the lives of multitudes.

THEORY OF CULTURE

Understanding culture is a significant dimension in the study of the characteristics of congregations. It requires a careful approach toward understanding the culture through which meanings are communicated. The humanistic disciplines have paid attention to the notion of culture in reference to popular forms of life incorporated within the range of notions including context, community, convention and norm.[1] The main goal of this research is to explore the culture of EECMY congregations that are engaged in holistic ministry and how emerging leaders are formed and empowered by those cultures. Therefore, the theory of culture provides a foundational framework for understanding the research interest.

The definition of culture has undergone considerable change through time. This change goes hand-in-hand with the development of theoretical approaches on how to understand people's culture. Among others, this researcher will use Clifford Geertz's interpretive tools on religion for the analysis of the dynamics that exists in EECMY congregations. More specifically, the researcher will use Geertz's understanding of sacred symbols in synthesizing people's ethos in African context.[2]

Among the books written by Geertz, *The Interpretation of Cultures*[3] displays his major contribution to the history of hermeneutics to that point. The primary purpose of this book is to find a satisfactory method for analyzing culture. According to Katrine Tanner, the term culture has evolved through different stages.[4] First, the term was most commonly used in Europe during the seventeenth, eighteenth, and nineteenth centuries to denote a sense of higher cultivated society or sophistication. Such understanding of the term culture carried with it the notion that a person, or a people, could strive to become more cultured through education and

---

1. Tanner, *Theories of Culture*, ix.

2. Geertz, *Interpretation of Cultures*, 89.

3. Geertz, *Interpretation of Cultures*, 89. The essays in this book deal with diversified subjects such as religion and ideology, ideology as cultural system, nationalism and politics, conceptions about time and identity, social and cultural process of change, and worldviews and sacred symbols.

4. For details, see Tanner, *Theories of Culture*.

self-discipline. Second, the definition of culture began to change in the early twentieth century and take on a more anthropological sense. The modern anthropologist now observed the culture of a people group from a supposedly objective distance. The term culture, in this anthropological sense, was a "group-differentiating, holistic, nonevaluative, and context-relative notion."[5]

Geertz was innovative twentieth century anthropologist who described culture from anthropological perspective. As Jason Springs rightly indicates, "one of Geertz's primary innovations [in his book *Interpretation of Cultures*] was to talk about 'culture' as a public, social context and set of relationships in and through which people interact meaningfully with one another."[6]

Geertz deals with methods in "analysis of cultures" based on "searching out of significant symbols, clusters of significant symbols, and clusters of clusters of significant symbols—the material vehicles of perception, emotion, and understanding—and the statement of the underlying regularities of human experience implicit in their formation."[7] For Geertz, this can be actualized through developing a "theory of culture" based on the "observable modes of thought."[8]

The term "observable modes of thought," according to Geertz, does not refer to forms of reductionism which attempt to analysis symbols based on the interest of social groupings or attempt to find out what is in people's minds.[9] Rather, for him, it refers to the purpose of cultural analysis, which is identification and interpretation of "clusters of symbolic acts" accompanied by "ferret[ing] out the unapparent import of things."[10] For Geertz, meaning is associated with human action placed into a context, and this context, as explained by Wim Hofstee, "is called culture and the social events it comprises can be described in such a way that their meaning becomes clear and comprehensible."[11]

5. Tanner, *Theories of Culture*, 24.

6. Springs, "What Cultural Theorists of Religion Have to Learn from Wittgenstein," 949.

7. Geertz, *Interpretation of Cultures*, 408.

8. Geertz, *Interpretation of Cultures*, 408, 418.

9. Geertz, *Interpretation of Cultures*, 18.

10. Geertz, *Interpretation of Cultures*, 26.

11. Hofstee, "Interpretation of Religion," 150.

Geertz defines culture as "a system of inherited conceptions expressed in symbolic forms by means of which human beings communicate, perpetuate and develop their knowledge about, and their attitudes towards life."[12] In other words, he describes culture as "a system of meanings embodied in symbols" within which human beings are provided with a frame of reference through which they understand reality and by virtue of which their actions are to be guided.[13]

For Geertz, symbols are anything that serve as vehicles for meaning, such as an act, a word, a ritual, an event, or an object. In his own words, symbols are "tangible formulations of notions, abstractions from experience fixed in perceptible forms, concrete embodiments of ideas, attitudes, judgments, longings, or beliefs."[14] Above all, symbols are "extrinsic sources of information."[15] In particular, when Geertz discusses Balinese cockfighting in his notes on *Deep Play*,[16] he develops his idea of reading cultural practices as "texts." He states that "the culture of a people is an ensemble of texts, themselves ensembles, which the anthropologist strains to read over the shoulders of those to whom they properly belong."[17]

Geertz defines religion as "a system of symbols which acts to establish powerful, persuasive, and long-lasting models and motivations in men by formulating conceptions of a general order of existence and clothing these conceptions with such an aura of factuality that the moods and motivations seem uniquely realistic."[18] Religious symbols, reiterates Geertz, "formulate a basic congruence between a particular style of life and a specific (if, most often, implicit) metaphysic, and in so doing sustain each with the borrowed authority of the other."[19] It is such articulation of religion and religious symbols that provides a significant framework for understanding the role symbols play in shaping the particular ethos (or how they motivate actions) of a given community.

According to Geertz, cultural acts are social events whose patterns transcend the boundaries of the individual and lie in the "intersubjective

---

12. Geertz, *Interpretation of Cultures*, 89.

13. Geertz, *Interpretation of Cultures*, 89.

14. Geertz, *Interpretation of Cultures*, 91.

15. Geertz, *Interpretation of Cultures*, 92.

16. See Geertz, *Deep Play*.

17. Geertz, *Interpretation of Cultures*, 452.

18. Geertz, "Religion as a Cultural System," 24.

19. Geertz, *Interpretation of Cultures*, 90.

world of common understandings into which all human individuals are born."[20] This world of common understanding is something not to be taken as an integrated and bounded system of symbols and meaning; instead, the "intersubjective" implies it is a paradigm or framework within which issues such as civil rights, gender, caste, and so on are dealt with.[21] As such, culture is an open-ended symbolic system in which people construct meaning and identity through "intersubjective" social interactions.

The method he proposes in interpreting such symbols begins with isolating cultural elements, which is then followed by identifying the internal relationships among these elements. The final stage he proposes is the general characterization of the whole system, based on one core idea around which other symbolic values are to be identified.[22] He makes a clear distinction between social structure and culture in such a way that culture is identified as patterns of meaning embedded in symbols, while social structure refers to as the "economic, political, and social relations among individuals and groups."[23] The overall process of describing and re-describing the symbols as a means to get at the embedded meaning is called "thick description." As Springs clarifies rightly, "the basic concept of 'thick description' is to interpretively discern and conceptually re-describe these socially instituted practices, and the norms implicit in those practices."[24]

The theory about culture is helpful for analyzing the concept of holistic ministry as understood by the EECMY congregations. The researcher intends to identify how congregations culturally understand life as a whole, and how such understanding guides their action. The sociologist Penny Edgell defines congregational cultures as "local understandings of identity and mission that can be understood analytically as bundles of core tasks and legitimate ways of doing things."[25] But the description of Roxburgh and Romanuk on the culture of congregations is more comprehensive: congregational culture is "how it [a congregation] views itself in relationship to the community, the values that shape how it does things, expectations of one another and of its leaders, unspoken codes about why it exists and who it

20. Geertz, *Interpretation of Culture*, 92.

21. Jodhka, *Community and Identities*, 13.

22. Geertz, *Interpretation of Cultures*, 17.

23. Geertz, *Interpretation of Cultures*, 362.

24. Springs, "What Cultural Theorists of Religion Have to Learn," 952.

25. Edgell, *Congregations in Conflict*, 7.

serves, how it reads Scripture, and how it forms a community."[26] The theory of culture as developed by Geertz is significant for the study of cultures of congregations mainly because, as emphasized by David Scotchmer, it "frees [the researcher] to interpret culture from within the real life experience and not outside it, as if we ourselves were hermeneutically sealed from it."[27]

THEORY OF LEADERSHIP

The focus of this research is to explore how emerging leaders are formed and empowered by congregations engaged in holistic ministry. To understand the "how" of leadership, the theory of leadership is foundational. Though leadership study has become popular among scholars, as Brien Smith et al., indicate, "There is still no comprehensive understanding of what leadership is, nor is there an agreement among different theorists on what good or effective leadership should be."[28]

There are three focus areas in the current studies on leadership. First, as G. Yukl rightly indicates, the current research on leadership has focused on leaders themselves.[29] Second, some research is also focused on context (or situations) within which leaders emerge.[30] Third, some research focuses on complex and dynamic processes happening in the relationship of leaders and followers (a focus area more related to the interest of this research).[31]

This research will use the theory of transformational leadership as a framework for understanding how followers (members of congregations) are formed and empowered (transformed) and become "transformational leaders." Transformational leadership theory fits this research because, as described by Skip Beli, it is a theory that focuses on leadership development (formation and empowerment) within the context of "continuing relationships of a relational community engaged in doing common works together."[32]

---

26. Roxburgh and Romanuk, *Missional Leader*, 63.

27. Scotchmer, "Symbols Become Us," 161.

28. Smith, Montagno, and Kuzmenko, "Transformational and Servant Leadership," 1.

29. Yukl, *Leadership in Organizations*.

30. Fiedler, *Theory of Leadership Effectiveness*.

31. Lichtenstein et al., "Complexity Leadership Theory." For Beli, for example, leadership is "a dynamic relational process in which people partner to achieve a common goal through service." See Beli, "Learning, Changing, and Doing," 95–96.

32. Beli, "Learning, Changing, and Doing," 95.

The term "transformational leadership" was first coined by J. Downtown in 1973, and was later used by MacGregor Burns in his seminal work *Leadership* published in 1978.[33] In this book, Burns laid down the foundation for transformational leadership, treating leadership as a process that occurs between the leader and the followers. In other words, he links the leadership role with that of the followers. With this approach, he introduced transformational leadership theory, a theory that diverted leadership studies from approaches focused on great leaders and transactional management to the interaction of leaders and followers as workers towards "mutual stimulation and elevation."[34]

Some studies have used transformational leadership and charismatic leadership as synonymous terms.[35] The two are, however, two separate theories.[36] As J. Hunt and J. Conger emphasize in their research, "there needs to be more differentiation between than there has typically been in the use of the two terms."[37] Therefore, this research follows the line of those who focus on transformational leadership in its own right.

Peter Northouse defines transformational leadership as "the process whereby a person engages with others and creates a connection that raises the level of motivation and morality in both the leader and the followers."[38] He also calls transformational leadership as "a socialized leadership, which is concerned with the collective good" of followers.[39] As Burns argues, "such leadership occurs when one or more persons engage with others in such a way that leaders and followers raise one another to higher levels of motivation and morality."[40]

Such an understanding about transformational leadership leads us, according to Burns, to a definition of leadership as a relationship of power for a specific purpose that is consistent with the motives, needs, and values

33. Burns, *Leadership*.

34. Burns, *Leadership*, 4. Burns' theory on transformational leadership has been the basis of more than four hundred doctoral dissertations.

35. Behling and McFillen, "Syncretical Model," 163–92; Conger and Kanungo, "Empowerment Process," 471–83.

36. To learn more about the difference between charismatic leadership and transformational leadership, refer to Miller, "Transformational Leadership and Mutuality," 180–92; Kanungo, "Empowerment Process," 471–83.

37. Hunt and Conger, "From Where We Sit," 340.

38. Northouse, *Leadership*, 4:176.

39. Northouse, *Leadership*, 5:172.

40. Burns, *Leadership*, 11.

of both the leader and the led. He states, "We must see power—and leadership—as not things but as *relationships*. We must analyze power in a context of human motives and physical constraints."[41] He argues, "Leadership mobilizes, naked power coerces. To be sure, leaders, unlike power holders, will have to adjust their purposes in advance to the motive bases of followers."[42]

Based on the above definition of leadership, Burns describes a transforming leader one who looks "for potential motives in followers, seeks to satisfy higher needs, and engages the full person of the follower."[43] This leads Burns toward the interest of focusing on the nature of *moral leadership*, which "emerges from, and always returns to, the fundamental wants and needs, aspirations, and values of the followers."[44] Northouse also portrays transformational leaders as those who "set out to empower followers and nurture them in change. They attempt to raise the consciousness in individuals and to get them to transcend their own self-interests for the sake of the others."[45]

As Beli states,

> Organizations are modified continually by the relationships going on as work is done. It follows then that the purpose of leadership development is not to train a person to perform a specific task in a certain way (competency), but to create within the person capacity to find within the work itself shared with a relational community potential for learning and growth.[46]

This theory is significant for this research because it provides a significant theoretical framework for understanding how emerging leaders are formed and empowered as leaders are involved in a relationship with their followers based on common purpose and collective needs. As Burns indicates, the key to leadership is the discerning of key values and motives of both the leader and follower and, in accordance to them, elevating (forming and empowering) others to a higher sense of performance, fulfillment, autonomy, and purpose.[47]

41. Burns, *Leadership*, 11.

42. Burns, *Leadership*, 43.

43. Burns, *Leadership*, 4, 20.

44. Burns, *Leadership*, 4, 20.

45. Northouse, *Leadership*, 190.

46. Beli, "Learning, Changing, and Doing," 95.

47. Burns, *Leadership*, 4.

Missional leadership (as explained in the first and third chapter of this research) pays careful attention to particular contexts and cultures where God is already at work. A missional church gives due consideration to transformational leadership in such a way that it nurtures the life and ministry of people with different spiritual gifts. The missional church always attempts to find a way to help them discern the values and purpose of their spiritual gifts. One major significance of transformational leadership is that it pays careful attention to talents and potentials in the followers, looking for a point of contact where meanings and purposes can be realized. In fact, the main emphasis of transformational leadership is not necessarily on the mechanism of an organization. Rather, it focuses on the common good of society.

SUMMARY

In this chapter, I selected two theories that give us keys to understanding the research interest, which is to explore how emerging leaders are formed and empowered by cultures of the EECMY congregations engaged in holistic ministry. There are three core areas addressed when exploring the research interest: leadership, cultures, and congregational ministries. As indicated above, the theory of culture is used as a framework to study the cultures of the EECMY congregations. The theory of leadership is used as a framework to study the process through which emerging leaders are formed and empowered by the congregations.

In the next chapter, I will define and describe the research methodology used to explore the research question. This research will utilize a simple exploratory method and qualitative approach. Additionally, each steps taken to explore the cultures of EECMY congregations using the methodology will be explained. The scope will be limited to Oromo speaking congregations within the vicinity of Addis Ababa, the capital city of Ethiopia.

Chapter 5

RESEARCH METHODOLOGY
AND DESIGN

INTRODUCTION

THE RESEARCHER HAS COME to the conviction that now is the time for "the return of the congregation to the study of theology."[1] This rationale follows the assumption that it is impossible to dissociate Christian life from Christian theology. Doing theology requires "attentiveness to specific people doing specific things together within a specific frame of shared meaning."[2]

In the previous chapter, I have described the two theoretical frameworks used in this research to explore the research question: cultural theory and leadership theory. These theories are helpful frameworks to explore the research question: How do cultures of the EECMY congregations that are engaged in holistic ministry form and empower missional leaders? Theory of culture helps to describe and define the cultures of the EECMY congregations. Leadership theory helps to analyze the process of formation and empowerment of leaders in the congregation.

In this chapter, I will discuss congregational study as a research paradigm, the research method and design used to explore the research question, and finally, ethical considerations. The first section describes congregational studies as a paradigm for studying congregational culture. The

1. Keifert, *Testing the Spirits*, 17.
2. Volf and Bass, *Practicing Theology*, 3.

second section will discuss the nature and purpose of the research methodology and data gathering techniques (including frames of analysis) used to explore the research question. The third section portrays the research design, which includes stages of data gathering, data analysis, and reporting. The final section discusses ethical considerations I was aware of and addressed at all stages of the research process.

STUDYING CONGREGATIONAL CULTURE

This study is mainly about exploring the cultures of the EECMY congregations engaged in holistic ministry and the impact of these cultures on the formation and empowerment of emerging leaders. The major question that needs to be discussed in this section is how to explore congregational cultures so that the methodology used as explained in the next sections becomes clearer. The field of study that explores the culture or practical nature of congregations within their social context is called congregational studies. Congregational study is founded on a "presupposition of the congregation's importance as a cultural and religious institution, and the effort to achieve empirically based understanding of the identity, effectiveness, and significance of the congregation within its wider social context."[3]

In congregational studies, the rich complexity and depth of congregational life is recognized. With this recognition, different methods of research such as participant observation, in-depth interviewing, and demographic and environmental studies are employed to study the natures of congregations in the study of religious communities and/or congregations. Congregational studies provide the framework for exploring the organizational dynamics and "local theologies" of certain religious communities.

What is the congregational culture that this research intends to explore? According to Ammerman, congregational culture is the congregation's "predictable pattern of who does what and a habitual strategies for telling the world about the things held most dear. [It] includes the congregation's history and stories of its heroes. It includes its symbols, rituals, and worldview."[4] Nancy Ramsay also similarly articulates congregational culture as "the congregation's story—its assumptions, its fears, its hopes. [It is the way a] congregation constructs reality—the way they see themselves,

---

3. Martin, "Congregational Studies and Critical Pedagogy," 122. See also Carroll, Dudley, and McKinney, *Handbook for Congregational Studies*, 7.

4. Ammerman, "Culture and Identity in the Congregation," 78.

their world, the nature of evil, and the character of God."[5] For Ramsay, congregational culture is a "living human document" that can be interpreted as a text.[6]

According to Ammerman, ways of exploring congregational culture should focus on the following three dimensions: *activities*, *artifacts*, and *accounts*. *Activities* refers to things the congregation does together, such as rituals, other activities (fellowship activities, decision making processes, education offered, or social gatherings, and so on). According to Ammerman, congregations create their culture, in large part, through the things they do together."[7] *Artifacts* are the things made by the congregation members (altars, buildings, holy books, the cross, and so on). *Accounts* are stories told to describe the congregation (which includes myths, history, language, worldviews, symbolic images, and metaphors, and theologies).[8]

Ammerman's proposal on how to explore congregational cultures is used in this research as a main frame. Particularly, the three dimensions that she presents (as described above) are used as main frames while coding and also analyzing the data. When describing the research finding in the next chapter (chapter 6), these three dimensions are categorized into two main sections: (1) congregational identity (who we are), which also subsumes *account* and *artifacts*, study of stories told by the congregation, theology, the artifacts, and things made by the congregation as the reflection of their identity, and (2) *activities* of the congregation (what we do together). These two categories used a means for analyzing congregational culture are described relation to their impact on the formation and empowerment of leaders.

5. Ramsay, "Congregation as a Culture," *Encounter*, 44.

6. Ramsay, "Congregation as a Culture," *Encounter*, 42.

7. Ammerman, "Culture and Identity in the Congregation," 84.

8. Ammerman, *Studying Congregations*, 78–129. According to James Hopewell, one way to explore congregational cultures is to study the "surprisingly rich idioms unique to each [and every congregation]," which is beyond the scope of this research. See Hopewell, *Congregation: Stories and Structures*. Dudley, McKinney, and Carrol also suggest the use of a cultural "frame" for exploring congregational cultures. See Carroll, Dudley, and McKinney, *Handbook for Congregational Studies*. This study will use "cultural frame" following the line of Nancy Ammerman.

RESEARCH METHODOLOGY

Before proceeding to discuss the research methodology employed, it is important to clarify a few terms that will be used throughout this chapter. According to John Creswell and Plano Clark, the term "methodology" is defined "as the [philosophical] framework that relates to the entire process of research."[9] Research design, on the other hand, refers to techniques of data collection and analysis such as "a quantitative standard instrument or a qualitative theme analysis of text data."[10] In other words, as explained by David De Vaus, research design is "a logical task undertaken to ensure that the evidence collected enables us to answer questions or to test theories as unambiguously as possible."[11]

The methodology adopted for this research is a qualitative simple exploratory methodology. Robert A. Stebbins defines exploratory research as a "broad-ranging, purposive, systematic, prearranged undertaking designed to maximize the discovery of generalizations leading to description and understanding of an area of social or psychological life."[12] Such explorations, he argues, "include descriptive facts, folk concepts, cultural artifacts, structural arrangements, social processes, and beliefs and belief systems."[13]

Exploratory research method is designed to explore, describe, and examine the social phenomenon or "individuals in social settings or examine the content of documents [by combining] a variety of observational, documentary, and interviewing tools."[14] As Rubin and Rubin explain, it focuses more "on understanding specific situations, individuals, groups, or moments in time that are important or revealing."[15] Using a qualitative simple exploratory method, the researcher was able to explore the culture of the EECMY congregations that are engaged in holistic ministry. Using this method was helpful to get a broader understanding of interviewees. This method was used in the process of discerning and discovering what God is up to in a particular context.

---

9. Creswell and Clark, *Designing and Conducting*, 4.
10. Creswell and Clark, *Designing and Conducting*, 4.
11. Vaus, *Research Design in Social Research*, 16.
12. Stebbins, *Exploratory Research in the Social Sciences*, 3.
13. Stebbins, *Exploratory Research in the Social Sciences*, 3.
14. Rubin and Rubin, *Qualitative Interviewing*, 2.
15. Rubin and Rubin, *Qualitative Interviewing*, 2.

Qualitative research involve various data gathering techniques (such as participant observation, in-depth qualitative interviewing, structured or unstructured conversation, document analysis, and field notes) that take seriously the human context of God's work in the world. These tools are identified under data gathering techniques bellow. Data gathered using these data gathering techniques are interpreted and analyzed to build themes and patterns.[16]

RATIONALE

This research adopted a qualitative research method rather than applying a quantitative or mixed approach. The researcher's choice of qualitative approach is due to the significant contribution and value it provides for the research. A qualitative approach is essential to explore the interest of this research for three reasons: First, as opposed to quantitative approaches, one of the strength of qualitative research methodology is the ability to explore events and activities in an in-depth manner.[17] As described above, the main interest of this research is to have an in-depth look into the dynamic processes of congregational life with the purpose to understand the cultural and theological perspectives of the studied congregations and processes of leadership formation. That means, the interests of this research have an exploratory quality since its focus is on the study of congregational culture. In order to fully explore the culture of congregations, a qualitative approach in which "the researcher seeks to establish the meaning of a phenomenon from the views of participants" is needed.[18] Qualitative method in which careful investigation, gathering of data through interviews, site visits, follow-up discussions, and clarifications were required.

Second, as described in the first chapter under "Review of Literatures," little research has been conducted to explore the main interest of this research in the Ethiopian context. As Croswell emphasized, qualitative

16. In recent years, there has been an "ethnographic turn" in ecclesiology, whereby numerous scholars have attended to the theological particularities of the local church. Qualitative data gathering techniques such as participant observation, in-depth interviewing, and structured or unstructured group conversation are used as ethnographic tools to study congregations. Though an "ethnographic turn" has some similarities with qualitative simple exploratory methods, this research will focus on the qualitative tools described above. For details, see Keifert, *We Are Here Now*.

17. Creswell, *Research Design*, 177.

18. Creswell, *Research Design*, 16.

approach is essential when "the topic has never been addressed with a certain sample or group of people."[19] One hope of this research is to contribute to start a missional church conversation in the African context and to engage the North American and European conversation on the missional church from an African perspective.

The third reason for choosing this methodology is mainly due to the philosophy or the assumptions behind the qualitative research methodology and data gathering techniques or research tools and its compatibility with the purpose of this research. According to Rubin and Rubin, there are two philosophical approaches to research: the positivist and naturalist-constructionist. The positivists claim is that there exists "a single, objective reality that can be observed and measured without bias using standardized instruments."[20] The positivists' goal is reaching a single conclusion using the same technique. In other words, they "seek to develop standardized instruments that they believe precisely tap a single reality."[21] The positivists use quantitative tools to measure or count and arrive at a single conclusion.

The naturalists, on the other hand, "accept that there is a reality but argue that it cannot be measured directly, but perceived by people, each of whom viewed it through the lens of his or her prior experience, knowledge, and expectations."[22] According to this philosophical approach, the people are the ones who build or interpret their external world, and the researcher's role is to explore and explain their viewpoints. Within the naturalist school of thought is the interpretive constructionism which emphasizes that meaning should be constructed out of "what people make of the world around them, how people interpret what they encounter, and how they assign meanings and values to events or objects."[23] They use techniques that contribute significantly to this research, such as participant observation, document analysis, conversational and narrative analysis, and in-depth interviewing. As Rubin and Rubin argue, the naturalist-constructionist

19. Creswell, *Research Design: Qualitative, Quantitative, and Mixed Method Approaches*, 18. Croswell also mentions that qualitative research is essential when the "existing theories do not apply with the particular sample or group under study." Since the interest of this research is not theory testing, the researcher is not considering this as one of the reasons for choosing a qualitative research approach.

20. Rubin and Rubin, *Qualitative Interviewing*, 15.

21. Rubin and Rubin, *Qualitative Interviewing*, 16.

22. Rubin and Rubin, *Qualitative Interviewing*, 15.

23. Rubin and Rubin, *Qualitative Interviewing*, 19. See also Sharan, *Qualitative Research*, 8–9.

approach provides several research techniques for cultural studies (such as this).[24]

DATA GATHERING TECHNIQUES

The researcher utilized three methods of collecting data: qualitative participant observation, in-depth interviewing, and qualitative documents. Qualitative participant observation, as Creswell articulates, is where the researcher "takes field notes on the behavior and activities of individuals at the research site."[25] According to Herbert Rubin and Irene Rubin, this technique of data collection helps the researcher "to sensitize [himself] to key issues, familiarize [himself] with the environment and language, and allows future interviewees to get to know [him] a bit before [he] start asking them questions."[26] The researcher's role in these activities should be relatively low, because, as suggested by Rubin and Rubin, such engagement "gives [the researcher] the opportunity to watch and take notes [and at the same time] minimize [his] influence on what is happening."[27]

Qualitative in-depth interviewing is where the researcher conducts face-to-face interviews with the participants. Qualitative interviewing is essential for exploring "in detail the experience, motives, and opinions of others and learn to see the world from" their perspective.[28] According to Rubin and Rubin, there are four basic types of qualitative interviewing: Internet interviews, casual conversations and in-passing clarifications, and sumi-structured and unstructured interviews.[29] Internet interviews are conducted using internet tools when the researcher is at a great distance from the interviewees. Casual conversation and in-passing clarification are interview techniques conducted while the researcher crosses paths with the interviewees. Semi-structured interviews are in-depth qualitative interviews focused on exploring a specific topic using pre-organized sets

24. Rubin and Rubin, *Qualitative Interviewing*, 26.

25. Creswell, *Research Design*, 181.

26. Rubin and Rubin, *Qualitative Interviewing*, 26.

27. Rubin and Rubin, *Qualitative Interviewing*, 26.

28. Rubin and Rubin, *Qualitative Interviewing*, 3.

29. Rubin and Rubin, *Qualitative Interviewing*, 29. There are also many other kinds of qualitative interviews in qualitative research ranging from informal conversation interviews to formal fixed-choice response interviews. See *Sage Handbook of Qualitative Research*.

of questions. Unstructured interview, on the other hand, are interviews conducted based on general topic to explore with an understanding that "questions are formulated as an interview proceeds."[30]

For this research, Casual conversation and clarification interviews were used as a method to collect data during participant observation. The main source of data gathered, however, were two semi-structured interviews conducted at each congregation: one in-depth interview with the leading pastor and one focus group conversation with ten participants from each congregations. The third data gathering technique was qualitative documents, which refers to documents collected during the interview such as minutes, reports, and budgets of the congregations.[31]

AN ACCOUNT OF RESEARCH DESIGN

As explained above, this research uses a qualitative simple exploratory method. Qualitative research is "a means for exploring and understanding the meaning individuals and groups ascribe to a social or human problem."[32] This research is designed with the theoretical assumption that congregational cultures have direct and indirect impacts on leadership formation and empowerment. Understanding the cultures of congregations requires an in-depth look into the dynamic processes of congregational life. In this section, I will discuss this process, which includes strategies or procedures of inquiry, specific methods and types of data collection, analysis, and interpretation.[33]

Congregation Selection

The research journey began with the selection of four EECMY congregations from which to gather data. The researcher used a three-stage discernment process to select interviewed congregations. To begin, criteria were needed to select five congregations that would contribute to the research interest of this project from among the many EECMY congregations that are engaged in holistic ministry. The researcher selected ten EECMY congregations

---

30. Rubin and Rubin, *Qualitative Interviewing*, 29–31.

31. Creswell, *Research Design*.

32. Creswell, *Research Design*, 4.

33. Creswell, *Research Design*, 3.

based on the following criteria: (1) churches that have been actively engaged in holistic ministry, means churches that are serving the spiritual (through ministries focused on evangelizing the unreached communities, worship, church education etc.) and the physical (through addressing the social, economic, and political) needs of the community, (2) churches that have been serving the community for over ten years, (3) Oromo-speaking congregations located in Addis Ababa, and (4) the recommendation of the EECMY Theology and Mission Board.

Second, the researcher created a preliminary list of these ten congregations, and mailed letters to each stating the purpose of the research project and inviting them to participate. Third, from the groups that responded (six congregations), the researcher conducted phone interviews with the lead and/or senior pastor to clarify the purpose of the study and the expectations of the congregations' participation, and then determined their availability within the given timeline of the research. Based on their responses, the researcher selected four congregations (Source of Life Church, Family Life Church, Love in Action Church, and Grace of God Church).[34] Besides their expectation and availability during the research time lime, the last criteria used during the phone conversation to select the four congregation was their context: The four that are selected, in one way or the other, are actively engaged in the spiritual, social, economic, and political life of the community they serve. Their ministry mainly concentrates on poor and marginalized people groups which are racially diverse but socially stratified, economically poor, and politically challenged.

Gathering Rich Data

In terms of data sources, the researcher collected data from the following five sources for each congregation: qualitative participant observation, casual conversation and in-passing conversation, one in-depth personal interview, one focus group conversation, and qualitative documents of each congregation. For the research, the in-depth personal interview and focus group conversation are the primary source of data, with the other data sources being supplementary. The researcher collected data from four

---

34. To maintain anonymity, the four EECMY congregations involved in the study received a pseudonym. Furthermore, generalized information is given for each congregation's identifying characteristics.

Oromo speaking EECMY congregations in Addis Ababa, Ethiopia, from July through October 2014.

The first phase of data gathering was qualitative participant observation. The researcher made an on-site visit over an extended weekend, recording what is seen and heard. The researcher's interest in the use of qualitative participant observation as one of the data gathering techniques developed out of the understanding that it is useful for observing people within their own cultural worldviews.[35] As a participant-observer, the researcher engaged each congregation in an on-site visit.

During the on-site visit, the researcher participated with and observed members of each congregation in their natural setting and attended as many activities as possible within the extended weekend. He participated in worship, staff gathering, congregational activities, social services and activities in relation to the neighborhood, and touring the congregation's local community. As Rubin and Rubin suggests, starting with participant observation was the key for the researcher's transition to the next stage of data gathering because it helped when "choosing interviewees as well as building sufficient trust to allow [the researcher] to interview them."[36] The researcher gathered field notes from the activities as well as from general observations and impressions while visiting the congregational sites.

The second phase of data gathering was qualitative interviewing. For this study, the researcher used casual conversations and in-passing clarifications during the first phase of data gathering, participant observation. Such interviews happen when the researcher and the interviewee cross paths and the researcher chats with the interviewee on topics relevant to the research.[37] The researcher had such brief moments with members of the congregation studied during which he was able to informally explore some issues related to the interest of the research. The primary data for this research was collected using semi-structured qualitative interviewing—an in-depth qualitative interviewing with one leading pastor at each congregation studied, followed by one focus group conversation consisting of ten participants at each congregation—which was hosted at each site.

Participants in the focus group conversation were recruited following the following criteria: (1) Those included in group conversation were members who had been involved in the congregation's local mission and/

35. Schwandt, *Qualitative Inquiry*.

36. Rubin and Rubin, *Qualitative Interviewing*, 61.

37. Rubin and Rubin, *Qualitative Interviewing*, 30–31.

or social services to the community for over three years, (2) referrals from the leading pastors (3), and gender balance. The interviews with the leading pastors lasted no longer than one hour and thirty minutes each. The group conversation, however, took between two hours and two and a half hours each. During the interviews, the researcher took field notes and memos on interviewees' attitudes and gestures or expressions. With the advanced permission of the interviewees, the researcher also video recorded these interviews.

The researcher utilized a protocol for interviewing the leaders and focus group participants.[38] The researcher designed two research protocols, one for the individual interview, and the other for focus group interviews. The protocols were designed with open-ended questions. According to Rubin and Rubin, open-ended questions are used to allow the interviewee to "respond any way he or she chooses, elaborating upon answers, disagreeing with questions, or raising new issues."[39] The researcher was also careful in making sure that the key questions and the follow-up questions asked were unambiguous and that they are significant in addressing the research interest. For this purpose, before interviewing the leaders and conducting structured group conversations, the researcher translated the questions into the Oromo language and field tested the protocols among two Oromo speaking congregations in Minnesota in order to ensure their clarity and appropriateness for the purpose of the research.

Upon field testing, the researcher determined the appropriateness of the interview protocols using the following criteria or principles as suggested by Rubin and Rubin: making sure that (1) the questions are clear to understand (2) the questions are interrelated, and (3) that "early questions do not restrict what the interviewees feel they can say later."[40] As they rightly indicated, presenting related and nonrestrictive questions to the interviewee results in a "richer and more detailed responses, since the interviewee are more likely to layer their answers."[41]

Based on the above three principles, protocols were designed in such a way that they helped gather rich data from the congregations. Four sections

---

38. See Appendix C and D.

39. Rubin and Rubin, *Qualitative Interviewing*, 29. Charmaz also advice the use of open-ended questions to focus the "interview questions to invite detailed discussion of the topic." See Charmaz, *Constructing Grounded Theory*, 65.

40. Rubin and Rubin, *Qualitative Interviewing*, 136.

41. Rubin and Rubin, *Qualitative Interviewing*, 136.

of questions were covered in both the personal interviews and focus group conversations. In each of the four sections, there were one or two probe questions asked to further explore the research interest. Probes are questions that follow the main questions for the purpose of "managing and, to a lesser extent, interpreting and clarifying the conversation."[42] The probes were used to allow enough space for additional and detailed accounts, a thick description, of the phenomenon under study.

The personal interview questions were focused on issues related to leadership. Leading pastors were interviewed to share their experience and explain how the cultures of the congregations form and empower missional leaders. This part of the interview was used to capture the formative experience of leaders. Questions designed for structured focus group conversations were used for the purpose of generating insights about congregations' self-identity and experiences of holistic ministry, and to explore what is happening in the formation and empowerment of leaders. Such an approach was also used to explore how theology emerges from within congregations, and how leaders are formed and empowered by congregations as the congregants reflect and act on those theologies.

Data Analysis

In terms of data analysis, the researcher followed Creswell's and Charmaz's steps of data analysis: organizing and preparing data (transcripts, field notes, images, etc.) for analysis, reading through all data, coding the data, summarizing themes and descriptions, interrelating themes and descriptions, and interpreting the meaning of these.[43] These stapes of data analysis were accomplished in three different stages.

First, one-and-a-half-hour interviews with leading pastors and between two-and-a-half hours focus group conversations (held at four of the elected congregations) were recorded, transcribed, and translated from Oromo to English. Because English is the second language of the researcher, the researcher hired an expert transcriber/auditor who knows and speaks Oromo and English for transcribing and translating the data. The expert also served in double-checking codes at the initial stage, line-by-line coding (see below the stages of coding employed).[44] The transcriber's input

42. Rubin and Rubin, *Qualitative Interviewing*, 139.

43. Creswell, *Research Design*; Charmaz, *Constructing Grounded Theory*.

44. See Appendix G.

in the initial stage of coding the data was essential since the researcher used *in vivo* coding, a coding system which required the use of words of the interviewees.

Second, the researcher carefully read through and reviewed the transcribed and translated data several times and compared it to the recorded interviews, field observations, and personal notes to ensure accuracy. The researcher consulted with both the transcriber/translator and the interviewee whenever the data seemed ambiguous. Reviving the transcribed/translated data also helped the researcher to familiarize himself with various forms of information provided by the interviewee. As he carefully evaluated the data, recurring themes, persons, symbols, and descriptions of certain events became more apparent.

Thirdly, the researcher analyzed the data using four levels of coding: (1) initial coding (line-by-line coding), (2) focused coding, (3) axial coding, and (4) theoretical coding.[45] I used *in vivo* coding on stages of line-by-line coding. *In vivo* coding, according to Charmaz, is a use of participants' "special terms as in vivo codes" in order to preserve the "meanings of their views and actions in the coding itself."[46] The use of *in vivo* codes allows the voice of those researched to be prioritized and honored. For *in vivo* coding, I used words or short phrases taken from each section of the data to identify patters. As Charmaz rightly indicates, line-by-line coding is helpful when our interest is to analyze "data [that] consists of interviews, observations, documents, or ethnographies and autobiographies."[47] Since this research involves the first three sources of data, it was vital to start with the line-by-line coding. This initial coding also provided an opportunity that allowed the researcher to double-check with the translator and the interviewees whenever the information seemed ambiguous. Such a process helped the researcher to understand the interviewees' point of view on a deeper level.

After initial line-by-line coding, focused coding was used to carefully go through the initial *in vivo* codes to determine which made the most analytic sense for categorizing the data into broader themes. This was done by comparing each *in vivo* codes with each other and the larger data. Some of the questions that the researcher considered while comparing the *in vivo* codes were the following: What is to be found when these codes are compared? "In which way might these codes reveal patterns? Which of

---

45. Charmaz, *Constructing Grounded Theory*.

46. Charmaz, *Constructing Grounded Theory*, 134.

47. Charmaz, *Constructing Grounded Theory*, 125.

these codes best account for the data? Do the focused codes reveal gap in the data?"[48] In other words, focused coding was utilized to synthesize and conceptualize larger pieces of the data.

The third coding phase was axial coding. The purpose of axial coding is "to sort, synthesize, and organize large amounts of data and reassemble them in ways after [focused coding]."[49] In axial coding, I further combined the focused codes based on the general relationship between the concepts which also helped the researcher identify the core practice of the studied congregations by allowing the categories from the focused codes to coalesce into major categories (axial codes).

The resulting axial codes were then compared through the next stage of coding process, theoretical coding. As indicated by Charmaz, theoretical coding are helpful for conceptualizing how the axial codes are related and moving the researcher's "analytical story in a theoretical direction."[50] This coding process was helpful to label ideas in such a way that it increasingly reflects theological perspectives that, one assorted, could be thematically-grouped into larger categories.[51]

ETHICAL CONSIDERATIONS

This research is mainly founded on sources of data obtained from conversational partners, face-to-face interview, with the leading pastors and ten focus group conversation participants of the four EECMY congregations. In order to protect conversational partners and insure confidentiality, it was essential to consider rigorous ethical considerations in every phase of the research.

The researcher paid careful attention to potential ethical issues in the process of the research as follows: first, the research proposal, which includes the designed protocols and all other procedures that the researcher intended to undertake, had to be approved by the Institutional Review Board (IRB) since it involved human subjects.[52] This process helped the

48. Charmaz, *Constructing Grounded Theory*, 140–141.

49. Charmaz, *Constructing Grounded Theory*, 147.

50. Charmaz, *Constructing Grounded Theory*, 150.

51. Charmaz, *Constructing Grounded Theory*, 50–60.

52. An Institutional Review Board (IRB) is a body charged with reviewing and approving all research proposals involved with human subjects. Since this research was conducted under the auspices of Luther Seminary, it had to be reviewed and approved

researcher improve some parts of his research protocol to avoid ethical issues that might arise as a result.

Second, each person participating in the interview was asked to sign an informed consent form before conducting the interviews.[53] The consent form highlighted the purpose and methodology of the study and clarified how the information would be used. The researcher also clarified to the participants the purpose and procedures of the interview. Third, surveys are filled out by each participants to anonymously provide his or her personal demographic information.[54] Fourth, a copy of the overall findings was promised to be made available to each congregation upon request.

Ethical issues also were avoided regarding data collection, analysis, and interpretation, and storage. To insure confidentiality, access to data was limited to the researcher and a scribe employed by the researcher. The scribe was made to sign a consent form in which he made an agreement to keep the information retrieved from the data confidential.[55] Upon completion of this research, the transcriptions and translated scripts from personal interviews and focused group conversations as well as the researcher's field notes and journal entries will be stored in a lock box and destroyed after seven years.

SUMMARY AND CONCLUSION

This chapter has provided the fundamental methodological framework that guided this research, describing the qualitative methodology used for this work and ethical considerations taken in the course of data collection, analysis, and reporting. The research employed a qualitative simple exploratory mothed designed to collect data to explore more in-depth the understanding and practice of congregational cultures and their impact on the formation and empowerment of leaders. Through qualitative interviews, utilizing both one-on-one interviews and group conversations, the researcher explored the influence of congregational cultures on emerging leaders. The next chapter presents the results from this study.

---

by the IRB of the Seminary.

53. See Appendix C and D.

54. See Appendix H.

55. See Appendix G.

Chapter 6

RESULTS OF THE STUDY AND INTERPRETATION

IN THE PREVIOUS CHAPTER, I have described the research method and design used to explore the research question. As indicated, a simple exploratory qualitative method was selected. This research was designed with the assumption that the cultures of congregations engaged in holistic ministry have direct contributions to the formation and empowerment of emerging leaders. There were four EECMY congregations selected for this research. All congregations selected for the study were Oromo-speaking congregations located in Addis Ababa, the capital city of Ethiopia.

One focus group conversation with ten members and an in-depth personal interview with a leading Pastor were conducted at each congregations from July to October, 2014. This makes forty-four total participants from all four congregations. The focus group conversation was conducted among four groups of people: elders (leaders of the congregation), deacons, youth and children ministry coordinators, and women ministry leaders. The youngest participants were in the age range fifteen to thirty (eight people in that age group), and the upper age group represented was sixty to seventy (two participants). In terms of gender, nineteen participants were female (43%) and twenty-six were male (57%). Most participants were in the age range of thirty-five to fifty (see Figure 1 below).

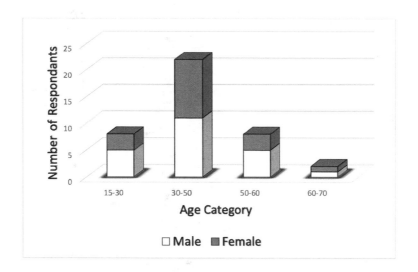

Figure 2: Respondents' Age and Gender Distribution

This chapter reports the findings from the visits to each congregation. Each report begins with a brief introduction to the congregation and summary of the research visit, followed by a report on the findings of group conversations and personal interviews conducted at each congregation and the resulting codes from the coding process. Finally, the responses of participants from each congregation are compared with one another to find cross-congregational similarities and differences.

In order to protect anonymity, the studied congregations and interview participants (both in qualitative personal interviews and focus group conversation) are given fictitious names. Numerous quotes appear throughout the report. They are from the transcript of the qualitative interview conducted at each congregation. The footnotes referring to these quotes are also anonymized for the same purpose.

SOURCE OF LIFE CHURCH

Source of Life Church[1] is the first Oromo-speaking congregation planted in Addis Ababa, the capital city of Ethiopia, in 1991. The church is located in a part of the city where most migrants from other cities in Ethiopia,

---

1. Names of churches and individuals are anonymized throughout this chapter.

particularly the Oromo, prefer to settle first due to its convenience. It is also a district where private and government schools and colleges are located. Along with these institutions, we find busy business centers.

When I walked into this congregation one Sunday, I was greeted by two women ushers. With a smile, they said *bagaa nagan manaa Waqaa dhuftee*, which means "Welcome to the house of God." I sat at the corner where I could view the congregation from a better angle. It was a huge tent. I was later informed that the tent was intended to be a short-term arrangement while the church expands attendance capacity in its permanent building—a project estimated for completion in two or three years. The tent can accommodate about two thousand five hundred people comfortably, and is well-equipped with modern amenities such as multimedia production and sound systems.

The demographic composition of the congregation suggests that younger people may feel more comfortable than older people. The church building, the dress code, and facilities within the church suggest that the majority of the members are young and poor (very few could be considered as among the middle class). Almost 60% of the congregation is under thirty years of age.

My impression from attending the worship service was that worship at this church focuses on the proclamation of the gospel, prayer for the sick and laying-on of hands, and how to help people to translate their faith into action. What is at the core of the preaching is biblical stories and testimonies used to empower members to caring for each other and others from outside the congregation or serving the greater community. The service, however, was spontaneous, allowing little order and structure. The pastor leading the worship was open towards participation of some members to pray and sing hymns whenever they felt like it, and cared less about the order or structure of liturgy. Praying for the sick and laying on of hands was also part of worship. The service lasted three to four hours. Members have described worship as "central to their congregation, both in shaping its identity and modeling their role in the community."

After Sunday church service, they have a fellowship time in which people participate with joy. Some Sundays (occasionally), they share bread and coffee while connecting with each other. They talk about what God is up to in their lives by sharing testimonies. The major part of their discussion is the word proclaimed on that specific worship service. People enjoy telling their stories in relation to the proclaimed word of the day.

What surprised me in visiting the Source of Life Church is that the church building is open every day, seven days a week, and there are different programs conducted on each day: prayer services, women's programs, youth programs, committee meetings, counseling services, and so on. The church continually opens her doors to the community.

The church actively participates in the day-to-day life of the community in many ways. Conducting and participating in weddings, funerals, and other social and community services is partly what makes her active in the life of the community. If there is anything going on in the community, Source of Life Church is always part of it. One community member observed, "This church is part and parcel of our community. It is part of our joy as well as our sorrow. We laugh and jump with joy with pastors. When we cry, we also cry together."[2]

The following text is written with bold letters at the gate of the congregation: "And I tell you that you are Peter, and on this rock I will build my church, and the gates of Hades will not overcome it" (Matt 16.18). When I asked why this text was put at the gate of the congregation, Pastor Matthew (the pastor of the congregation) stated that it is because the text describes the true identity of a church, and that their congregation aspires to identify itself within that text. When I asked his understanding of the text, he stated that "the rock in which the church is founded is the word of God. Once the church is founded on God's word, there is nothing in this world that can overcome it. Therefore, the church is able to take part in God's mission."[3]

The role of pastors in the Source of Life congregation is to coordinate the ministries of the congregation, provide education (confirmation classes, discipleship class, all ministers' occasional training, and so on), lead worship (occasionally), and provide counselling services. Their other main job is to challenge and motivate members to participate in the ministries of the congregation. Except for leading liturgy and administering sacraments, the primary mechanisms for caring out all other ministries have always resided in the lay ministers.

Qualitative Data from Source of Life Church

I conducted one focused group conversation with ten members from the Source of Life congregation who are involved in different kinds of ministries.

2. A community member observer

3. Interview with Pastor Matthew, see appendix B.

I also conducted a one-on-one interview with the leading pastor of the congregation who holds the primary position in leadership. Fifty-nine *in vivo* codes emerged during the analysis of the interview with the focus group, and thirty *in vivo* codes emerged out of the one-on-one interview with the pastor.[4] These *in vivo* codes were merged together and grouped into thirteen focused codes. The twelve focused codes were identified from what all the participants shared commonly, which were once again combined to form four axial codes.

Table 1. Source of Life Church Axial and Focus Codes

Axial Codes	Focused codes
• Creating a Bible-centered worshiping community and a mother church with emphasis on worship	• Becoming a Bible-centered church • Worshiping community of believers • A mother church
• Serving the whole person	• Healing ministry • Evangelistic ministry • Strong outreach • Advocacy • Development projects
• Adopting values of African culture for leadership and ministry	• Oromo cultural values • African traditional religion
• Leadership formation and empowerment	• Leadership development • Discipleship ministry • Women, children, and youth empowerment

Table 3 above illustrates the connection between the axial and focused codes. The axial codes that emerged can be summed up with four key words: *worship, holistic, cultural,* and *leadership formation.* The finding of the research showed that the Source of Life church describes its identity and ministry with emphasis on *worship.* To be a *worshiping* community is the core identity and aspiration of the congregation. Every activity of the congregation, which is *holistic* in nature, happens in, with, though, and by the *worship* life of believers.

4. See Appendix F.

74

Culture or African cultural values set a context for both the fellowship and holistic ministry. The church's concept of *holistic ministry* emerges both from its cultural understanding of a human person as a whole and its theological conviction. Interview participants have indicated with emphasis that for them as Africans, it is impossible to dissociate the humanitarian or development and spiritual services they provide for their members as well as the wider community. They also argued that their understanding about holistic ministry does not contradict with their faith, but is rather affirmed by it.

Leadership formation, on the other hand, is a process impacted by African *cultural values*, the congregation's identity (with emphasis on *worship*), and the congregation's practical *holistic* engagement. The research indicated that leaders emerge within the context of the congregation's internal and external activities. Internal activities are activities that take place within the four walls of the congregation, such as worship, education, etc. External activities are different ways (social, economic, political) in which the congregation engages the community.

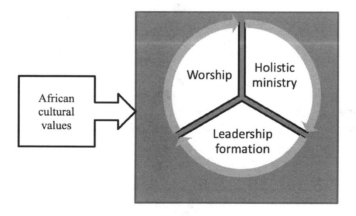

Figure 3: Axial Codes of Source of Life Church

As indicated in figure 3 above, the research showed that each of the axial codes are interconnected in such a way that the concept of leadership formation cannot be properly understand and described without identifying and analyzing the interconnection between the four axial codes (*worship, holistic ministry, cultural values,* and *leadership formation*). The identity of the congregation, *worship,* informs the activity of the congregation, which is *holistic*. *Leadership formation*, on the other hand, refers to the formation process of emerging leaders within the context of *worshiping* community that is engaged in *holistic* ministry. For a missional church as a worshiping community that is engaged in holistic ministry to exist, there needs to be a missional leader—a leader *formed* and *empowered* by congregational ministries.

Based on the key words in axial codes, what we can understand about the Source of Life Church (its theoretical code) is that its main value or objective is to be a Bible-centered worshiping community of believers that works for the spiritual development of its members (leadership formation and empowerment) and serving others holistically. Worship is at the core of its identity, and serving the whole person is its mission. Both the core identity of the congregation as a worshiping community and its holistic activity (both informed by African cultural values) provide a scenario within which emerging leaders are formed. Below, I present a summary of an analytical description of the congregation based the identified axial codes: its identity (*worshiping community*), activity (*holistic ministry*), *cultural values*, and the praxis of the congregation in relation to *leadership formation*.

Worshiping Community

As described above, *worship* is one of the axial codes identified during analysis of the research data. During the group's conversation, when I asked their view of the church, they responded by asserting that a church is a worshiping community of believers founded on the word of God. When I asked how they describe their congregation, they asserted that it is a Bible-centered worshiping community of believers. The Bible is proclaimed as the foundation for Christian faith and living. They made statements such as "we are worshiping community," "Bible believing members," "our faith and praxis is founded on Bible," and "we are Bible-centered worshiping community."[5]

When explaining how their understanding of their congregation as a worshiping community (informed by their Bible-centered life and ministry) is expressed in the life of the congregation, they talked about formal Sunday school classes, Bible studies organized in villages, and discipleship classes and other formal education programs they use to educate and equip their members with the word of God and how that informs their worship

5. See Appendix E for an overview of group conversations at Source of Life Church.

life. One of the interviewees, a Bible study coordinator of the congregation, stated that she "has not seen anything like the excitement and development in peoples' lives when engaged in weekly Bible study programs organized by the church."[6]

When asked what members of the congregation think regarding the identity of their congregation, they stated that members of the congregation have a similar understanding about their identity as a Bible-centered worshiping community. A man, however, added that members also describe themselves as *Waldaa Hadhaa*, a "mother church,"[7] and others in the group nodded with agreement. I asked for explanation, and he said,

> This church is a mother church to tens of Oromo speaking congregations planted in different parts of the country. By reaching the unreached, it gives birth to new congregations and nurtures them until they are fit to support themselves. This activity of the church emanates from its identity as a worshiping community. Therefore, the word "mother church" has two implications for the people: that the church gives birth to new congregations by focusing on evangelism and that it also nurtures the evangelized community like a mother to be a worshiping community of believers.[8]

When describing their church as *Waldaa Hadhaa*, I observed excitement and pride on the face of those in the group conversation. They like telling their story of the past years with passion. These are the years in which they were able to plant tens of Oromo-speaking congregations throughout the country and how they continued to follow-up with the newly planted congregations' progress. They assert that "the congregation's call is not only to evangelize and plant congregations, but also to follow-up with the progress as a mother church."[9] The congregation allocates more than 40% of its budget to outreach programs aimed at starting congregations in places where the church does not exist. Sometimes they also start outreach programs based on enquiries from Oromo-speaking Christians who have little support to start a new congregation. Since the start of this congregation,

6. See Appendix E for an overview of group conversations at Source of Life Church, Participant F.

7. See Appendix E for an overview of group conversations at Source of Life Church, Participant I.

8. See Appendix E for an overview of group conversations at Source of Life Church, Participant I.

9. See Appendix E., Source of Life Church, Participant B, D, and F.

through these types of outreach programs, several new congregations have been planted.

Holistic Ministry

Holistic ministry is one of the axial codes identified during the analysis of the research data. This code emerged from a qualitative interview question that was focused on exploring the contributions of the Source of Life Church in its community. Those in group conversation agreed that Source of Life Church is committed to helping the community with practical needs. They explained that the congregation refers to this compassionate act as diaconal service. Every two years, organizers for diaconal service are elected from among active members responsible for mobilizing each member for diaconal service. Mobilizing activities include "developing projects for community service, raising funds, selecting skilled people for practical implementation of the project, and follow up of the projects."[10]

The two kinds of support that are usually provided by this congregation are food and clothing. Through coordinated efforts, Source of Life Church offers assistance to the community in its neighborhood. They also provide training on sanitation and are engaged in cleaning services. They provide training to the local poor to become entrepreneurs, producing small stand-alone sanitation treatment systems and cleaning public areas that are of danger to the community due to unsanitary conditions and poor hygiene.

Source of Life Church, partnering with other congregations of the EECMY, also actively participates in awareness programs with regard to advocacy, health, and domestic violence. They implement the motto of Peace Office, an office of the EECMY established to coordinate the work of advocacy at the national level, at the local level. The congregation also help members develop capacity to engage in advocacy through education. One of the church elders during the focus group conversation mentioned that "the church wants its members to have a strong prophetic voice in society in general."[11] When asked how the church makes this practical, he asserted that the congregation provides education on "the responsibility of Christians in politics and economy," education aimed at helping members understand that Christianity is not all about spiritual activities, and is about

10. Appendix E, Source of Life Church, Participant C.
11. Appendix E, Source of Life Church, Participant J.

every aspect of human life.[12] The congregation, however, is neutral when it comes to politics.

When asked how this contribution is influenced by faith, a woman responded that "Every member of our congregation is committed to serving the community because they believe that this is part of their mission. As a worshiping community, we are called to address the physical and the spiritual needs of our people. That is our public worship (Mark 10:45)."[13] In this congregation, community services are always accompanied by spiritual services, and vise versa.

The other activity carried out by the congregation in the community it serves is evangelism. Leaders of Source of Life congregation argue that they do evangelism "through direct proclamation, social work, religious education, and services."[14] They assert that their evangelistic approach is holistic, and that this has been the reason why tremendous growth of membership has been registered since the congregation was established. They also cooperate with other churches and organizations in the area to reach the unreached.

After pastors', evangelists', and administrators' salaries, they allocate most of their budget to outreach programs. Outreach programs are aimed at the work of evangelism with a holistic approach. For example, when the congregation plans to do evangelism among the unreached community in a given village or town, they engage that given community in multiple ways, including proclamation and development (opening schools or starting water pump projects, and so on). Evangelists are recruited as missionaries and are sent to cities where non-Christians are mostly allocated.

Currently, the Source of Life Church has fourteen outreach programs in different parts of the country. The objective is to help these outreach programs develop into a congregation. An outreach programs turns into a full-fledged congregation when it has more than twenty-five members and is able to govern and support itself financially. When planting a congregation, they mostly build new worship centers, and sometimes rent houses until the new congregation is able to build its own worship center.

I asked why they as a congregation, care about their own community and the community at large? What motivates them? Some responded to the questions by referring to faith. "Faith in this congregation," they asserted,

12. Appendix E, Source of Life Church, Participant J.

13. Appendix E, Source of Life Church, Participant A.

14. Appendix E, Source of Life Church, Participant C, E, H, J.

"is an active faith. It is an active faith because it has to be expressed in practical terms."[15] Several people talked about how their faith is related to their call to serve others. They quote the following verse: "What good is it, my brothers and sisters, if you say you have faith but do not have works?" (Jas 2:14). Good works, they assert, "means living out our faith within and outside our Christian community. We understand that we are saved not by good works, but by faith in Jesus Christ, but we also believe that our faith becomes meaningless if not expressed in practical terms through our worship life and Christian ministries."[16]

Leadership: Empowering Ministries

Leadership formation is an axial code identified during analysis of the research data. This code emerged due to a qualitative research question that was aimed at exploring how the congregational life and identity shape or empower future leaders. During the interviews, some people talked about how Bible-centered teaching resulted on the formation and empowerment of leaders. The congregation's emphasis on education and Bible studies that are meant to equip members for ministry have a major impact in equipping leaders. Others referred to the culture of shared leadership as a means for leaders to emerge and to be empowered. They stated, "In this congregation, leadership is widely distributed and shared. Pastors and evangelists see themselves as direction setters, but those involved in ministry [almost all members] see themselves as equippers. It is not long after a new member joins the congregation that he/she starts sharing in leadership in some capacity."[17]

One educated woman added that the culture of fellowship among members also has an impact on leadership empowerment. Members of Source of Life Church are highly motivated for worship and ministry, stating "It is engraved into the hearts of believers that come together to worship as well as to minister to one another and to the community at large on a regular basis. They hunger to be in each other's lives."[18] For her, this plays out in worship together as a church, as they treat each other as brothers

15. Appendix E, Source of Life Church, Participant A, C, D, E, I.

16. Appendix E, Source of Life Church, Participant A, C, D, E, I

17. Appendix E, Source of Life Church, Participant A, C, D, E, I

18. Appendix E, Source of Life Church, Participant D.

and sisters, how they respond to the needs of the community, and how members form and empower each other as leaders.

The practice of leadership formation in the Source of Life Church was explored more in personal interview with Pastor Matthew, a pastor of Source of Life Church. In the interview, Pastor Matthew described a leader as "someone who takes the responsibility he/she is entrusted by the community to help his followers achieve their goals."[19] He stated that a leader is only a leader when "he/she has followers and there exists a goal or a destination towards which he/she aspires to lead his/her followers."[20] According to him, leadership should be understood in terms of the relationship that exists between a leader or leaders and the followers, and their aspiration to reach for a common goal.[21]

When asked what is required to be a leader, Pastor Matthew answered by stating that leadership requires the ability to form or create a system or culture of shared leadership. For him, leadership in Africa can only be carried out as a community. Decisions are made as a community. Church activities, even in the pastoral office (except sacraments), are carried out in collaboration with lay members. Therefore, it is required of a leader to always be open to share responsibilities, and allow every member of the community to be part of both decision making and other ministries of the church.[22]

When asked what members of his congregation think about the role and responsibility of a leader, Pastor Matthew immediately responded by referring to the ecclesial trend of EECMY congregations and African traditional worldviews as holistic. He stated that the EECMY's approach to ministry "does not compartmentalizes the Christian faith and relegate the application of Christianity solely to the spiritual dimension of people."[23] This understanding, according to Pastor Matthew, has an impact on what the EECMY member's think about the role and responsibility of leaders. He stated that the EECMY member's think of their leaders as having a responsibility and role "that goes beyond internal activities of the congregations such as leading worship, facilitating fellowship among members, etc."[24]

19. Interview with Pastor Matthew.
20. Interview with Pastor Matthew.
21. Interview with Pastor Matthew.
22. Interview with Pastor Matthew.
23. Interview with Pastor Matthew.
24. Interview with Pastor Matthew.

When asked to tell biblical stories used in his congregation to describe a leader, he quoted from John 10:1, 11, and 14, where Jesus refers to himself as a "good shepherd." This image, according to Pastor Matthew, is compatible with the African understanding of what it means to be a good and exemplary leader. More importantly, the comparison between a "good shepherd" and a bad shepherd or a thief in John provides a good image of good and bad leadership.[25]

According to Pastor Matthew, the other image used more often in his congregation is servant leadership.[26] When Jesus said "whoever desires to be great among you, let him be your servant" (Matt 20:26, Mark 10:45), he was showing his disciples that leadership is not about being great, but about being a servant. His washing of the disciples' feet at the last supper is a good example for this. Such a leader would place his followers' interests ahead of his/her own.[27]

How are leaders raised in your congregation? He stated that every member is gifted in different ways. Therefore, every believer is given an opportunity to participate in ministry. For him, "the EECMY's tradition of giving each believer the opportunity to serve regardless of his/her age and ministerial position is what enables leaders to emerge, and to grow in service. The EECMY congregations understand that all members are ministers. Whether a pastor or lay ministers, we are all called to serve."[28] He paused for a moment, pulled a text from the Bible (1 Cor 12:7), and read out loud "to each is given the manifestation of the Spirit for the common good."

He added, "It is in the process of involving every member in ministry (ministry of all believers), where equal opportunity is created for all members to serve each other, that leaders emerge because such a process is where they grow in faith. Prayer programs and Bible studies organized in villages are especially effective places for leaders to emerge because our members serve each other on a regular basis. It is at places where we have our fellowship, whether within the church or in villages and public places, that leaders emerge."[29] He paused for a moment, pulled a text from the Bible

25. Interview with Pastor Matthew.
26. Interview with Pastor Matthew.
27. Interview with Pastor Matthew.
28. Interview with Pastor Matthew.
29. Interview with Pastor Matthew.

(1 Cor 14:26), and stated, fellowship places are where we "let all things be done for building up."

I asked a follow-up question: What are this congregation's contributions in the formation and empowering leaders? He stated that "formation and empowerment happen mainly in a context where believers are in fellowship with God and with each other. Our fellowship is founded on our worship life. That is also why the church exists: to enable all human beings and the creation to be in harmonious fellowship with God, and to enable every human beings to be in fellowship with each other and the whole of creation."[30]

There are several activities that take place within and outside this congregation. Whatever the congregation does, they do it as a community. As the pastor emphasized, "it is in their worship life and in their communal endeavors to engage in God's mission that they are formed into the likeness of Christ."[31] The major activity of the congregation is worship. Through preaching of the word and administration of sacraments, people grow and are rooted in faith. This is spiritual formation experienced through fellowship with God and our fellow brothers and sisters.[32]

The congregation also has children's ministry (Sunday schools) where children learn from adults and also from each other. Like adults, they have their own worship service. They have children's choirs, program leaders, and so on. The young adults also have separate programs where they pray and study the word of God together. As the pastor explained, they "have different classes for teaching members at different stages such as confirmation classes and discipleship classes. Prayer groups and Bible study groups are also organized in villages where most members live."[33] Again, he turned to the Bible and quoted Ephesians 4:11–12: "the gifts he gave were that some would be apostles, some prophets, some evangelists, some pastors and teachers, to equip the saints for the work of ministry, for building up the body of Christ."

30. Interview with Pastor Matthew.
31. Interview with Pastor Matthew.
32. Interview with Pastor Matthew.
33. Interview with Pastor Matthew.

African Cultural Values

African cultural values was identified as one of the axial codes identified during the analysis of the research data. Participants of group conversation as well as Pastor Matthew (in personal interview) agreed that the congregation's identity as well as activities are shaped by African cultural values. They also indicated that the cultural values have impact on the formation and empowerment process of leaders.

Pastor Matthew asserted that the culture of the congregation is related to its identity as Lutheran and member's ethnic and cultural background. He stated, "As a Lutheran congregation, members have their own tradition that makes them different from other denominations. As an Oromo-speaking congregation, it is also different from those speaking other languages. All our members are from the Oromo tribe. This also makes us distinct from multi-cultural and multi-lingual congregations."[34]

He continued, "As Lutherans, our worship service is focused on proclamation of the word and administration of sacraments. As Oromos, we also have our cultural values and concepts reflected as a culture of our congregation."[35] He also indicated that the use of vernacular languages in worship, song, sermon, teaching, prayer, conversation, and so on has its own impact in forming our cultural identity. The pre-Christian religious experience and rich cultural heritage that the Oromo believers entertain, as long as they do not contradict with Christian faith, also has its impact on ways emerging leaders are formed.[36]

When describing the impact of cultural values on leadership formation, participants of group conversation indicated that a cultural languages or images, *Lubaa*, is used to describe a leader (which influences how the congregation understands leadership). Pastor Matthew also stated the Oromo use of the term *Lubaa*, which means "a Pastor," is taken from the traditional Oromo designated name for leaders.[37] The *Lubaa*, in Oromo tradition, is a chosen leader responsible mainly for rituals, but who also plays judicial and advisory roles. The *Lubaa* is a practical expression of God's blessing. He is believed to have the power to deliver blessings as well as curses. When evangelical Christianity was introduced among the Oromo

34. Interview with Pastor Matthew.
35. Interview with Pastor Matthew.
36. Interview with Pastor Matthew.
37. Interview with Pastor Matthew.

by the missionaries, the traditional name *Lubaa* was given to ordained pastors, by virtue of which the believing community continued to uphold the pastors (*Luboota*, the plural of *Lubaa*) as leaders in all realms of life.

FAMILY LIFE CHURCH

Family Life Church was founded at the outskirts of Addis Ababa, in the suburbs. It is about a twenty-five minute drive from the center of the city. It had been a decade since my last visit to the congregation. A lot of change has happened since then. Driving from the center of Addis Ababa, where I reside, towards this congregation was not easy. There was major railroad construction going on by a Chinese company. I had to use an alternative temporary road constructed for public use until the completion of the construction.

The face of this place has changed dramatically in the last decade. The small suburb I knew is now engulfed by huge buildings functioning as business centers, hotels, colleges, and so on. It was a suburb where many poor, working-class people lived back then. But now it is a suburb where the poor as well as wealthy live. It has become a reflection of the true face of the economic system of the country which continues to increase the wealth of a few rich people and burden the poor to survive with the least available income.

This suburb is a place where "failures of political and economic systems have led to the deterioration of the basic necessities of life."[38] In the year I conducted my research, people living in this area, particularly the Oromo, were constantly demonstrating for their rights. The Family Life Church, surrounded by people victimized by the system, attempts to be a caring place so that people will find "a place they can call home, and sisters/brothers they can call a family."[39]

When I walked into the congregation's compound the first time, I was astonished by what I saw. The congregation owns about twelve acres of land. Besides a small congregation built in a European style of church building, they have an elementary and junior high school serving the community. The large green area, with extremely beautiful flowers when in full bloom and trees, is eye-catching and colorful. Walking inside the church compound was utterly delightful.

38. Appendix E, Family Life Church, Participant J.
39. Appendix E, Family Life Church, Participant J.

The Sunday worship is a blend of both traditional and modern. The leading pastor starts with liturgy, followed by singing and praise with traditional and modern music, proclamation of the word, prayer and laying-on of hands for the sick, and ends with the blessing of the pastor. The liturgy is adopted from the European Lutheran churches and the Ethiopian Orthodox Church traditions. The hymn book they use is a translation of European songs translated to Oromo by Onesimos Nesib in the 1890s. They also sing contemporary Oromo songs. It is interesting to observe them standing straight while singing from a hymn book, and dancing with joy when singing the modern songs. The preaching is solid and relevant. In prayer, people connect with each other and with God at the same time.

The worship service is similar to the Pentecostal church's worship style in many ways, but also takes the Lutheran form of Liturgy. In fact, it is a mix of both. They do liturgy like mainline Lutheran churches, and pray like Pentecostal Christians. A woman from the congregation asserted, "Such tradition is what we are. We are Lutherans in doctrine and tradition, but we are also charismatics in our prayer and worship practice. The two are a perfect mix."[40]

African communal culture is adopted by the Family Life Church to help identify their identity as a community of believers. Their sense of community is what guides their activities. It is out of its identification of itself as a community (with members of the congregation and others) that it focuses on offering its hospitality to everyone in need, within and outside the congregation.

Qualitative Data from Family Life Church

I conducted one focus group conversation and one face-to-face interview at the Family Life Church. Ten participants were involved in the focus group conversation. These participants were serving actively in different types of ministry. The face-to-face interview was conducted with the pastor, Pastor Mark, who holds a leading position in the congregation.[41] Thirty-seven *in vivo* codes emerged during the analysis of the conversation with the focus group of Family Life Church.

40. Appendix E, Family Life Church, Participant F.
41. All named in this chapter are anonymized.

During the analysis of the personal interview with Mark, the leading pastor of the Family Life Church, twenty-one *in vivo* codes emerged.[42] These were combined into ten focused codes, which were then combined into four axial codes. Each axial code was supported by a number of focused codes. Table 4 below illustrates the connection between the focused and axial codes.

Table 2. Family Life Church Axial and Focus Codes

Axial Code	Focused Codes
Spirit-led community of believers that focuses on offering hospitality to the people it serves	• Identified as a community offering hospitality • Self-definition as a Spirit-led church
Holistic public engagement with emphasis on evangelism	• Engaged in welcoming the community • Focus on community service, holistic approach • Evangelistic ministry
Faith tradition and practice shaped by African traditional values	• African traditional values • Oromo communal practice
Church practices and teachings that lead to spiritual development and leadership formation	• Discipleship formation in small-group ministry • Spiritual development • Leadership formation

The first axial code refers to how the Family Life Church identifies itself in relation to God's mission, for which it exists. *Hospitality* is at the heart of the church's self-description. *Holistic ministry* (serving the whole person) describes the congregation's activities, activities that make no distinction between the spiritual and the physical. The focus of these activities, however, is *evangelism.* When it says "focus," it is a matter of prioritization which emanated from an understanding that development or addressing human needs begin with spiritual transformation—which then leads to social and material transformation. It is the self-description and activities of the church that has direct implication on *spiritual development* and *leadership formation* processes that happen in the church. Overall, the church's self-identification and praxis is shaped by *African cultural values.*

42. See appendix F.

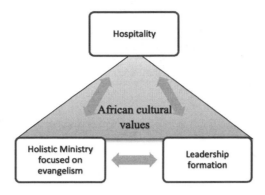

Figure 4: Axial Codes of Family Life Church

Figure 4 above shows the relationships between the axial codes. As described in the figure, all axial codes are interrelated in a way that all axial codes inform each other. The identity of the church (*hospitality*) is informed by the *African cultural values*, the activities of the congregation (*holistic ministry*), and its leadership praxis. The more significant finding of this research is that the identity of the congregation and its activity (which are both informed by *African cultural values*) have a direct impact on the formative experience of emerging leaders.

This way, the axial codes were brought into conversation with one another, creating theoretical codes. A closer look at the axial codes leads to the following theoretical code: emerging leaders in the Family Life Church are formed and empowered in the context where the church defines its identity as a church that offers hospitality and is engaged in culturally informed practices of holistic ministry with an emphasis on evangelism. Below, I present a summary of an analytical description of the congregation based on the identified axial codes: its identity (a church offering *hospitality*), activity (*holistic ministry*), and the praxis of the congregation in relation to *leadership formation*.

Hospitality

Hospitality is one of the axial codes that emerged during the analysis of the research data collected from the Family Life Church. During the focus group conversation, when asked the congregation's view of the church, some used words such as "family church," "my family," and "a mother church" in responding to the question.[43] Some also talked about the church as a place to make connection and offer hospitality to others. They stated, "the church defines itself through Jesus' command to His disciples to go and make disciples (Matt 28:19). The church is a sent community, sent to evangelize and make disciples through making connections and offering hospitality."[44]

The congregation's focus on offering hospitality to the community it serves is reasonable when seen from the perspective of the context. Because of the political and economic situation, the people living in the neighborhood of the congregation are vulnerable to multi-faceted economic and social problems. The Family Life Church offers its assistance and hospitality and attempts to make the people feel welcomed as a member of the family.

The Family Life Church describes its hospitality to others as the work of the Holy Spirit in their life and ministry. They said, "We are a Spirit-led church that offers hospitality for all of God's creation."[45] They understand that all their ministries within and outside the congregation are guided by the Holy Spirit. They continually talk about discerning how the Spirit is moving among them and among the community they serve, and, in fact, the whole world. For them, God is alive in the midst of everything that happens around them. They assert that the church is only able to serve others when it participates in what God is up to in this world.

Holistic Ministry

The third axial code that emerged during the analysis of research data collected from the Family Life Church is holistic ministry. The Family Life Church has created a welcoming and accepting community which many members have enjoyed. They keep their arms open wide to everyone interested in joining them. Their hospitality catches people as they first encounter this community. It is such encounters that invite many into a deeper discipleship journey with other members of the congregation. On my last visit to this congregation, during fellowship time after church service, a women said to me "I come to this church with my children because this is

---

43. See Appendix E, Family Life Church.

44. Appendix E, Family Life Church, Participant B, C, and H.

45. Appendix E, Family Life Church, Participant B, C, and H.

the place where I feel at home. I feel like I have sisters and brothers who love me, care for me and my kids."[46]

The Family Life Church members express their desires to seek out people in need and to allow themselves as a community to become hospitable for everybody. When I asked about the contributions of this congregation in this community, some asserted that the congregation is engaged in a wide range of community activities. They have a community school, well projects, women's empowerment projects, counseling services, and so on. They run child sponsorship programs, partnering with a humanitarian organization named Holistic Ministry of Children of the Horn of Africa (HMCHA).

They also have a "donkey project" in which they buy and provide donkeys to women in the area to relieve them from having to carry heavy loads on their backs while fetching water and carrying goods from the market. They buy donkeys and distribute them to women in villages. This ministry saves women from a lot of hard work which endangers their lives.

Some in the group also added that the Family Life Church is known for its focus on family ministry.[47] They run a strong family ministry. They provide pre-marital counseling, and marriage and family teaching for couples. These ministries are offered both for church members and interested people from the community. It is this ministry that mainly connects members together, and serves as a link between the congregation and the community.

Evangelism

Evangelism is the major activity of the congregation. Perhaps, other activities of the congregation are all "carried out to support the evangelistic role of the congregation among the community."[48] Many talk about how evangelism becomes effective when supported by other ministries of the church such as development and social activities (as mentioned above).

When asked how this contribution is influenced by faith, an elderly woman responded with a slow voice that this is how God's mission is carried out through the church. She said, "As Christians, we are called to be a witness to our community. To be a witness, you have to be in service. And

46. Appendix E, Family Life Church, Participant F.

47. Appendix E, Family Life Church, Participant C, D, I, J.

48. Appendix E, Family Life Church, Participant H.

when you service, you do it holistically, you serve the physical as well as the spiritual aspects of the community."[49]

The woman's response moved us to the other activity of the Family Life Church in the community. Another person added that this church is also committed in evangelism. "Perhaps," he said, "members are inspired by their conviction of reaching the unreached with the good news of the gospel. They believe that the church is founded on Jesus' command to his disciples to go and preach the good news to all the nations and make them Disciples of Christ (Matt 28:19). They see this command in conformity with Jesus' healing and prophetic ministry."[50]

They informed me that the congregation has fifteen outreach areas yet to grow to becoming a congregation. In these outreach areas, the congregation provides holistic service to the community it aims to evangelize. Schools, water pump projects, medical services, and financial support to those who intend to start small businesses are some of the support provided at these outreach sites.

African Cultural Values

The other axial code that emerged during the analysis of the research data is *African cultural values*. This axial code emerged in relation questions asked with an intention of exploring the influence of African culture or values on how they understand themselves as a church and their leadership practice. All group conversation participants agreed that cultural values shape the congregation's identity, its ministries, and its understanding and practice of leadership.

For example, when asked what cultural languages or images are used to describe a church, one woman, referring to the text in Isaiah 57:7 ("My house will be called a house of prayer for all nations"), stated that the term *manaa ummaata*, a home for nations, is used by church members to show hospitality for others.[51] Others in the group agreed with her description of the church as *manaa ummaata* and asserted that a home for nations is a metaphor used by leaders and members of the congregation on

---

49. Appendix E, Family Life Church, Participant E.
50. Appendix E, Family Life Church, Participant I.
51. Appendix E, Family Life Church, Participant E.

several occasions to describe the identity of the congregation in terms of its hospitality.[52]

When Pastor Mark was asked about what cultural languages or images are used to describe a leader, he asserted that there are different terminologies used in the Oromo language to describe a leader. The work *raaga* is used to refer to a leader with a prophetic gift. Such a person is also described as *waa argaa* (seer) or *waa dhagawaa* (voice hearer). These terms are used to describe leaders as those who can envision the future, and lead their people towards envisioned goals.[53] These terms are borrowed from Oromo traditional religion (OTR). In OTR, some people, particularly gifted leaders, can communicate with the creator from inside "this world;" the creator is supposed to be from the other side of the world. Such an understanding was adopted by the church context to describe leaders as having the gift to communicate with God, and are therefore seers (*raaga*) and voice hearers (*waa dhagawaa*). The *Waaqa* (God) appears to these leaders in vision, dreams, and augury.

Leadership: Empowering Ministries

Leadership formation is the fourth axial code that emerged during the analysis of the data collected from the Family Life Church. Every member in the Family Life Church is part of the leadership. What distinguishes the pastor's role from other members is his ordination, which allows him/her to lead liturgy and administer sacraments. Otherwise, all members are welcome to participate in other ministries of the church, and the pastor is simply a facilitator to several ministries functioning under the pastoral office.

When I asked how leaders are raised in this congregation, the chairperson of the elders committee, who participated in the group conversation, explained as follows. In the Family Life Church, pastors and evangelists are the primary teachers. Under their supervision, there are many volunteer teachers involved in teaching in different ministries, such as Sunday school, Bible study, youth ministry, and women ministry. In fact, most leadership activities are carried out by lay ministers. "It is such a leadership tradition that created an opportunity for leaders to emerge, and for members of the church to empower each other as they aspire to serve one another and

52. Appendix E, Family Life Church, Participant A, D, E, G, M.
53. Appendix E, Family Life Church, Participant A, D, E, G, M.

others. It also gave each member the confidence in their own abilities and gifts to minister to each other."[54]

I asked how the congregational life and identity shape or empower future leaders. A man stated that there are two concepts that highlight the peoples' commitment towards empowering each other's lives. First, small groups organized within the congregations play a vital role in creating a conducive atmosphere for leaders to emerge. Second, village programs provide the opportunity for people to come together and support each other for spiritual formation and growth.[55]

Some talked about the hospitality of the congregation and its impact on emerging leaders. They said fostering a culture of hospitality has helped them to be a church that nurtures and empowers its members as well as the community in many ways. Lay ministers, especially the women and the youth, have a dynamic, inviting, and welcoming spirit.[56] They invite their community regardless of differences in religion, ethnicity, culture, and so on, and they welcome them with joy. The welcoming spirit within this community is both evangelical and educational. This dynamic is forming and empowering both members of the congregation and the community they serve.

The practice of leadership formation in the Source of Life Church was explored more in personal interview with Pastor Mark, a pastor of Family Life Church. When I asked his understanding of a leader, Pastor Mark stated that a leader is "someone who nurtures his followers to grow. A leader focuses on developing people with humility. A leader is also someone who has high level of interpersonal skills and integrity."[57]

I asked a follow-up question, what is required to be a leader? Pastor Mark stated that a leader (in a church context) has to be matured in faith and experience. Maturity and experience can be summarized as wisdom in leadership. So wisdom is required to be a good leader. Leadership also requires determination, creativity, flexibility, preparedness to be challenged at all time, willingness to listen to others, and the skill (gift) to teach and develop others.[58]

---

54. Appendix E, Family Life Church, Participant A, B, G, I, J.

55. Appendix E, Family Life Church, Participant A, B, G, I, J.

56. Appendix E, Family Life Church, Participant B, F, J.

57. Pastor Mark. See Appendix B.

58. Pastor Mark.

When asked what members of his congregation think about the role and responsibility of a leader, Pastor Mark stated that the expectation of members of his congregation from leaders is based on what they need in life, both spiritually and physically. He asserted that most members are economically poor, socially discriminated against due to their ethnicity, and are politically challenged. Therefore, they expect their leader to be someone who can help them go through all these challenges.[59]

I urged him to say more, and he continued: The EECMY was first established among the poor and the marginalized people. These people are the Oromo and other nations and nationalities from the southern part of Ethiopia. It was the EECMY that preached good news to these communities, established schools, hospitals, and other development centers that helped these people to progress both in terms of self-esteem (in which faith played a major part), economics, education, and so on. This is the legacy of this church under the leadership of pastors, evangelists, and lay ministers. Members of the EECMY want this tradition to continue, and therefore think that pastors have the responsibility to follow such a tradition by engaging every life the community they serve.[60]

When asked to tell biblical stories used in his congregation to describe a leader, pastor Mark stated that Jesus' sharing with his disciples, the time that he took to teach them and disciple them, is emphasized as a prime example for teaching about leadership. His compassionate life towards the poor and marginalized, his prophetic ministry being voice for the voiceless, his authoritative teaching, and his self-giving commitment to his followers are emphasized in his teaching about leadership.[61]

I next asked how leaders are raised in the congregation. The pastor indicated that the congregation has different kinds of services, such as the regular Sunday service, women's ministries, young adult ministries, children's ministries (Sunday school), and ministers' programs. These are regular services that take place every week (except for ministers' programs). Outside the congregation, members organize prayer programs and Bible studies in villages. According to him, "village programs have significant contribution in members' lives because that is the place where fellowship

59. Pastor Mark.

60. Pastor Mark.

61. Pastor Mark.

is strengthened (intimacy among members is created), and members learn from each other how to apply Christian faith in their day-to-day lives."[62]

Secondly, as the pastor states, the congregation members are active in reaching out to the community in multiple ways. They participate in cleaning the streets and villages, they own the community school, have water projects where they dig walls to make water available for their community, and they run other development programs in which the members actively participate. They participate by envisioning the projects, allocating funds, running the programs, and reflecting on the outcomes.[63]

I asked a follow-up question: What are this congregation's contributions in the formation and empowering leaders? Pastor Mark asserted that the formation happens in multiple ways. First, the spiritual activities that take place within the congregations and in villages (prayer and Bible studies) are aimed at enriching the life of our members. We want members to be well-rooted spiritually. Second, when members are engaged in community service, they experience the joy and suffering of others by participating in their daily lives "by practically showing their love and care for the community, they impact others, and are also impacted by others. It is such experience that results in formation of leaders."[64]

As the pastor argues, he had observed leaders growing out of such experience. Some developed their leadership skill through such experience and have become inspirational leaders in congregations, some became committed workers in government offices, and others work for Non-Governmental Organizations (NGOs).[65] When asked how the culture of the congregation is related to the formation and empowerment of leaders, Pastor Mark asserted that his congregation's culture has to be viewed from three perspectives. First, since it is an Oromo-speaking congregation, Oromo culture is reflected in the way decisions are made, worship is conducted, and members communicate with each other.

Second, it is a Lutheran congregation. There are certain elements (worship and leadership styles) and theological positions that make Lutheran congregations different from other evangelical, Orthodox, and Catholic congregations in Ethiopia. Third, the congregation, like many other evangelical congregations in Ethiopia, is also influenced by charismatic

---

62. Pastor Mark.
63. Pastor Mark.
64. Pastor Mark..
65. Pastor Mark.

practices. They give room to gifts of the Holy Spirit such as healing, prophecy, and others in worship services.[66]

LOVE IN ACTION CHURCH

Love in Action Church was started as an outreach of the Source of Life Church in 1992. It became a congregation in 2002, with about membership of fifty people. At present, the congregation has about two thousand five hundred active members. The congregation is located at the business center of Addis Ababa. International hotels, malls, and the biggest airport in Ethiopia are located in this area. Therefore, people living in this area are mainly rich business people, foreigners, and government officials. There are some from the middle income community who manage to live in this area.

My first visit to the Love in Action Church was a surprise. It was a surprise because everyone I saw until I entered the church compound were Muslim Somalis. I could observe several shops and restaurants around the congregation, and most of them were owned by the Somali community. The restaurants and shops have Somali names, and people walking on the streets to get to these places were speaking Somali, and were dressed in traditional Arab fashion.

There were about two thousand five hundred people worshiping on Sunday morning. Most members of the congregation were dressed in Oromo cultural clothing. Most members are young, between eighteen to thirty years of age. Later in my conversation with church members, I was informed that most of these young members of the congregation are students of Addis Ababa University, the biggest university in Addis.

At Love in Action Church, worship is central. Worship is offered in two styles, traditional and contemporary. They do not allocate different times for these styles of service, but rather, meld both styles together in one Sunday morning service. Worship starts mostly with traditional liturgy followed by contemporary cultural style of worship, or the other way around.

The preaching touches every life of the community. I could observe preachers trying to connect the Bible message with that of the day-to-day life of the people. Their style of music, which is taken from Oromo traditional styles, is what reaches to a deeper place within the heart of the people. The worship leaders wear Oromo traditional clothes. Pastors leading liturgy, however, are dressed with typical western Lutheran pastors' robes.

66. Pastor Mark.

Qualitative Data from Love in Action Church

Like the three congregations described above, I conducted a focused group conversation with ten active members and a personal interview with the leading pastor of the Love in Action church, Pastor Luke. Thirty-five *in vivo* codes emerged during the analysis of the focused group conversation with the Love in Action Church ministers and seventeen *in vivo* codes emerged during the analysis of the interview with Pastor Luke, the leading pastor of the church.[67] These *in vivo* codes were merged and grouped into eleven focused codes, which then underwent another level of abstraction, creating four axial codes.

Table 3. Love in Action Church Axial and Focus Codes

Axial codes	Focused codes
Understand themselves as a faith-based worshiping community that aspires to be a "community of disciples"	Worship is central to the identity of the church. Have a mission of creating a "community of disciples" Have firm understanding that their action is influenced by their faith.
Focus on serving the whole person.	Serving the whole person Demonstrate strong public ministry.
Demonstrate faith in African context by upholding the traditional worship culture and communal values.	Value the Oromo worship culture, *Waaqeffanna* Uphold African communal culture
Facilitate the formation and empowerment of leaders through practicing shared leadership and raising awareness in emerging leaders.	Intentionally engaged in leadership formation and empowerment Focus on small-group Bible study and prayer programs Exercise shared leadership. Develop awareness in emerging leaders.

Table 5, above, illustrates the connection between axial and focused codes. The first two axial codes indicate the self-identification of the Love in Action Church and the action that emerges from it. There are three characteristics identified as to how this church describes itself: *faith based*, *worshiping community*, and *a community of disciples*. The interrelationship between these characteristics is put in a way that one character leads to the

67. See Appendix F.

other character: faith of the community leading to true worship, and faith-based worship leading to the formation of *a community of disciples*.

The action that emerged from a church that identified itself as *a community of disciples* is holistic ministry. Following the Scriptural and African cultural understanding of humanity as both physical and Spiritual, their ministry is defined as *holistic. African cultural values* create the context within which the church constructs its self-identity, participates in God's mission, and *leadership formation* happens.

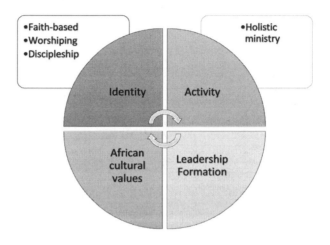

Figure 5: Axial Codes of Love in Action Church

Figure 5 illustrates the connection between axial codes in the form of theoretical codes. The arrows indicate the interconnectedness of the four axial codes. The Love in Action Church is focused on its self-identification and mission, which is a faith-based *worshiping community* aimed at creating a *community of disciples*. Its self-identification informs its activities, which are *holistic*, and vise versa. The *African cultural values*, on the other hand, inform the identity as well as the activities of the congregation. This leads to the following theoretical code identified by the research: The Love in Action Church is a culturally informed faith-based worshiping community of disciples engaged in serving the whole person. Below, I present a brief summary of an analytical description of the congregation based on the identified axial codes.

Faith-Based Worshiping Community of Disciples

Faith-based worshiping community of disciples is one of the axial codes identified during the analysis of qualitative data collected from Love in Action Church. *Worship* is central to the ministry of the Love in Action Church. According to one of the members of the church council, "everything the church does emanates from her worship life. Perhaps, all her activities are part and parcel of her worship life." They consider all church services (and fellowship) and activities of the church within their community as connected. They talk about activities of members within and outside the church as the outflow of their worship life.

When asked what members of the congregation think about regarding the identity of a church, some used words such as "worshiping community," "fellowship," or "family" to describe what the church meant to them.[68] Others talked about the church as a *community of disciples*, a place where disciples are made by being formed into the likeness of Christ.[69] Still others used a language of service. In the mission statement of the church, it is indicated that the church "aspires to be a community of disciples."[70] For them, a church is established to be the means through which members reach out to the unreached communities through holistic ministry. Many, however, emphasized worship as central to the identity of the church.[71]

When asked what biblical stories or passages they use to describe a church, I was surprised to hear many referring to the book of Acts, particularly Acts 2:42: "And they devoted themselves to the apostles' teaching and the fellowship, to the breaking of bread and the prayers."[72] As Lutherans, they understand the church as a place where the word of God is preached according to the "apostles' teaching" and sacraments administered (the breaking of the bread and fellowship with God and fellow brothers and sisters happen).

---

68. See Appendix E, Love in Action Church, Participant A, B, D, I.

69. See Appendix E, Love in Action Church, Participant C and H.

70. Mission statement of the Love in Action Church

71. Appendix E, Love in Action Church.

72. Appendix E, Love in Action Church

Holistic Ministry

Holistic ministry is one of the axial codes that emerged during the analysis of qualitative data. Love in Action Church organizes multiple programs weekly in which members as well as invited guests from the community participate. I have participated in a coffee ceremony occasionally organized after Sunday service, and have observed how people have fun together and enjoy each other. It is a time for hugs and smiles and connection. Here, the people are comforted in companionship while breaking bread together. I have also participated when organizers were raising funds for a diaconal program on this occasion.

Outside the church, members are also connected through social networks and spiritual programs that help in villages, such as Bible study and prayer programs. I once participated in a Bible study run weekly by few members of the congregation. There were fifteen of them in the group, five men and ten women. It was lively! Everybody partook with eagerness to know more. When asked the significance of Bible study groups and prayer programs organized by the congregation, a women asserted that "it connects members of the congregation to come together and enrich each other with the word of God and pray for each other. It also connects members to other people living in villages with their neighbors. It is another way of connecting with our neighbors by inviting them to pray and study Bible with us."[73]

I asked members about what their congregation contributed to the community. Those I interviewed asserted that their congregation was thoroughly embedded in the community. Their community service is based on the needs of the people they serve. Leaders' main roles are to "evaluate those needs and use the mutual leadership culture of the congregation while setting priorities, praying for discernments, and discussing with church members before making decisions."[74]

This congregation works on AIDS outreach in villages, through which it attempts to transform the sexual life of the community. Members who are health-care professionals take the lead in this program. The congregation has small clinics built at different locations to help the community get health-care. They also have water projects, small-scale business training

---

73. Appendix E, Love in Action Church, Participant E.
74. Appendix E, Love in Action Church, Participant C.

and capacity building projects, and educational support projects (particularly for orphaned children).

They also spoke out on the discrimination of women and harmful traditional practices such us female genital mutilation. Ethnic-based discrimination is also another social problem regularly addressed by this congregation. A woman once asserted that "this congregation does not shy away from challenging the community on social and economic matters when the time demands."[75]

The congregation is also committed in evangelism work. They are inspired and willing to share the good news of the gospel in multiple directions. Fifty congregations grew out of the support of Love in Action Church. At present, they have twenty-seven outreach areas. The congregation's way of planting congregations is by starting outreach areas that gradually develop into congregations when they are able to support themselves in all aspects.

At this congregation, evangelism is mainly carried out in prayer programs held in villages. The women, in particular, are joyful in sharing the good news with their neighbors through inviting them to prayer programs conducted in villages. A woman said to me, "Signs and wonders that happen during our time of prayer are what draw people to Jesus. They see what He is up to in our lives, then they get eager to have Him touch their lives as well. That is how I became a Christian. That is how most of us became followers of Jesus."[76]

In the last fourteen years of its existence as a congregation, through its evangelism and outreach ministry, fifty other congregations were founded in different parts of the country. At present, the congregation has twenty-seven outreach ministries expected to grow into congregations. Love in Action Church runs all the twenty-seven outreaches with its own budget, allocating evangelists and pastors to serve them.

I asked how their contribution is influenced by faith. Some stated that they "understand community service as an extension of their faith and as an opportunity offered to them by God."[77] They describe their commitment to community based on their understanding of *missio Dei* at work in the community. They believe God is up to something within their own

75. Appendix E, Love in Action Church, Participant E.
76. Appendix E, Love in Action Church, Participant H.
77. Appendix E, Love in Action Church, Participant A, E, G.

community of faith and within the lives of the people there. Therefore, they assert, "to reach out to the community is to follow God's footsteps."[78]

Their understanding of *missio Dei* at work is based on both pre-Christian Oromo tradition (*hojii Waqaa ummaa*, the work of God the creator) and biblical understanding of God's ongoing creative work in our world. Several people have talked about how *Waqaa* (God) is active in their lives and ministry, and how *Waqaa* is present in their community as well.

When asked about their involvement in the community, one man asserted that

> As Oromo, it is our tradition to help each other as a community, and those that are outsiders. Before we became Christians, we consider such practice as obligatory to each member of the community. This how God created us. We said this is the work of God the creator (*hojii Waqaa ummaa*). After becoming Christians, the Bible affirmed our prior understanding. We now understand that it is no more about us helping each other, but it is God reaching out to the community through us as his vessels.[79]

African Cultural Values

The other axial code that emerged is *African cultural values*. This axial code emerged as a result of qualitative questions asked to explore the significance of African cultural value in how the congregation understands itself and its ministry. All participants in the group conversation agree that the identity of their congregation and its ministry are all informed by these cultural values. The interesting experience in the Love in Action Church is their willingness to let the Oromo traditional ways of being community become transformed into new informal ways of being together as Christians. Their worship, fellowship, public engagement, and the way they describe themselves (their identity) are all framed by their understanding of what it means to be a Christian as African indigenous people, as Oromo.

During focus group conversation, when I asked cultural languages or images are used to describe a church, many talked about the Oromo culture of *waaqeffanna* as having connection with their view of the church as a worshiping community.[80] *Waaqeffanna* is African traditional religion

78. Appendix E, Love in Action Church, Participant A, E, G.

79. Appendix E, Love in Action Church, Participant D.

80. Appendix E, Love in Action Church, Participant D.

practiced among the Oromo. The Oromo word *waaqeffanna* is translated as "worship," but is also used as synonymous term with religion. According to one educated man in the congregation, "It is long before the Oromo became Christians that they identified themselves as *waaqeffatta* (worshiping community)."[81] He explains as follows: "*Waaqeffanna* was our traditional religion, and we defined ourselves as *waaqeffatta*. After becoming Christians, we came to the understanding that Christianity is also a call to be *waaqeffatta*, but this time to be a waaqeffatta of the one true God."[82]

When I asked Pastor Luke about what cultural language or images are used to describe a leader, he asserted that the word *Qaalluu* and *Abaa Gadaa* are used to describe a leader. In Oromo Traditional Religion (OTR), the spiritual leader is called *qaalluu*. *Qaalluu* is the highest spiritual leader , and plays significant role in keeping peace and stability, and provides security to those who are under his leadership.[83] In OTR, the highest form of leadership is given to *Abaa Gadaa*. *Abaa Gadaa* is also responsible for the socio-economic, socio-cultural, and socio-political affairs of the community. *Qaalluu*, on the other hand, is a spiritual leader who also has authority over ethical and cultural matters.

Leadership Formation

Leadership formation is one of the axial codes that emerged during the analysis of qualitative data collected from Love in Action Church. The Love in Action Church is active in empowering people for ministry and helping people understand God through deep Bible teaching. The leadership is aware of the peoples' desire and eagerness to learn the word of God. They continually invite people to learn and be challenged by the Scriptures. The pastors and evangelists are the primary teachers, but they also invite teachers from other congregations and theological seminaries.

Their young members want to be engaged intellectually as well as spiritually. One of my observations was young members organizing a theological discussion forum on the relationship between Christianity and politics, inviting intellectuals from higher institutions. The discussion was well-organized, open for everyone to participate, and constructive in many ways.

81. Appendix E, Love in Action Church, Participant I.
82. Appendix E, Love in Action Church, Participant I.
83. Appendix E, Love in Action Church, Participant I.

When asked how leaders are raised in this congregation, and the role faith has in leadership development, many talked about the different stages of educational programs, starting from Sunday school for children to discipleship programs organized for adults, as favorable grounds from which leaders emerge, and as gradual stages of leadership formation. As a women commented, "When planning and conducting these educational programs, the congregation aims at enriching children, youth, and adults to emerge as leaders and serve each other and the community with better preparedness and knowledge."[84] The congregation gives attention to helping people both learn the basics of Christianity and to work through what it means to be people with living faith. They believe that God is at work within this community through such ministries, and hence, He will tend to the growing.

I asked how congregational life and identity shape or empower future leaders. Some also talked about formation and empowerment of leaders when involved in actual ministry as a community. The practice of shared leadership that allows all members to participate in all areas of church service "has become informal practical training whereby many are mentored on how to lead a group, engage the community, work in partnership, and so on."[85]

Others asserted that formation and empowerment of leaders mainly happen in small-group ministries. Members take time to pray together, share the word of God, and serve each other and others in small-group ministries. Members gather in small-groups to pray and study the Bible. Such practice is important for the life and ministry of every member as they continually seek to be open to the guidance and works of the Holy Spirit. Small-group ministries are "carried out by lay ministers, and its leadership is shared among all who participate regardless of age and gender. Prayer programs, and Bible studies in particular, are foundational for overall activities of the congregation, including leadership. They are foundational for the formation and empowerment of leaders."[86]

The practice of leadership formation in Love in Action Church was explored more in personal interview with the pastor of the church named Pastor Luke. When I asked his understanding of a leader. Pastor Luke asserted that leadership (in a church context) requires a discovery of a sense of call to serve others. Calling has to come first, and it has to be understood

84. Appendix E, Love in Action Church, Participant F.
85. Appendix E, Love in Action Church, Participant A, B, G, J.
86. Appendix E, Love in Action Church, Participant A, B, G, J.

that it is a call to serve everybody in the community (those inside the church and outside the church circle). A leader is also someone committed to shared leadership. Leadership in the African context is all about the capability to transfer power to everybody in a community. A leader is someone who is committed to building communities, and able to transfer responsibility and accountability to community members at all levels. This is how a leader is able to make a difference in people's lives.[87]

The follow-up question was, "what is required to be a leader?" Pastor Luke asserted that leadership requires rootedness in spirituality, wisdom, and commitment to serving the community in all aspects of life. The leader has to know the cultural values of the people he/she is leading. Leadership also requires persevering dedication, trustworthiness, and skills, among other things.[88]

When asked what members of his congregation think about the role and responsibility of a leader, Pastor Luke asserted that members expect their leader to be committed to building community and shared leadership in addressing both the spiritual and physical needs of the community. They expect from their leaders a sense of intimacy with the community he or she is leading, willingness to share responsibilities, and readiness to give emotional support and affection.[89]

When asked to tell biblical stories used in his congregation to describe a leader, Pastor Luke asserted that the life and ministry of Jesus is emphasized as a good model of leadership. From Jesus' leadership, his self-description as the good shepherd who lays down his life for his sheep demonstrates his deep commitment to his followers (John 10:15). Jesus' description of servant leadership (John 13:1–5), a leader who is even committed to serving his followers to the extent of washing their feet, is also emphasized, along with others.[90]

The follow-up question was, "what are this congregation's contributions in the formation and empowering of leaders?" Pastor Luke stated that "it is the dynamics of socialization and the transformation inherent in the process where congregational members are engaged in ministry that functions as a significant means through which leaders are formed

87. Pastor Luke, see Appendix B.
88. Pastor Luke
89. Pastor Luke.
90. Pastor Luke.

and empowered."[91] In spiritual services organized inside the church, such as preaching of the word and administration of sacraments, members are formed. The fellowship among believers by itself, whether they are inside the church or outside, had an immense impact on the formation of leaders. In ministries of the church conducted outside the church, such as development activities, evangelism, outreach ministry, and so on, leaders are formed while practically trying to live out their faith.[92]

GRACE OF GOD CHURCH

The Grace of God Church began as an outreach program by the Source of Life Church in 1992, and was organized as a congregation in 1994. It is located in a fast-growing urban community. Most of its members came from Amharic speaking congregations due to conflict over language as well as forms of worship. The Amharic speaking congregations were not willing to allow other languages and cultures to be used in worship services, for they believed and argued that plurality in languages and forms of worship would finally result in division and conflict rather than unity.

The Grace of God Church is in a suburban setting which transitioned into an urban area within a short period of time. It has a strategic piece of land at the intersection between the big urban population in Addis Ababa and gradually developing villages at the outskirt of the city. By establishing outreach centers at both locations, the congregation aims at ministering to both the over-populated urban town and the slowly progressing villages of the city.

The congregation is planted on a small piece of land, approximately four thousand square feet. The building has two levels. The first level is the sanctuary. The second level is partly the sanctuary, with a few offices for the pastor and other activities. The congregation's building is located between houses, with which it shares fences. The congregation's effort to acquire land was turned down by the Ethiopian government, which forced members to consider buying a house and turning it into a congregation.

When walking into the congregation, I was greeted by two women ushers. They were both dressed in Oromo traditional clothing. I sat in the middle of the congregation. There were about five hundred worshipers all together. Most members are young. From their dressing style, I could

91. Pastor Luke.
92. Pastor Luke.

determine that most members are from the middle class, while there are also some from poor economic backgrounds. Children were actively participating in the worship service.

At the Grace of God Church, worship is central and is a melding together of traditional and contemporary worship elements. Worship starts with a traditional liturgy and hymns (adopted from traditions of European missionaries and the EOC) and gradually moves to the contemporary (like contemporary Oromo hymns and visual images). Proclamation of the word, singing hymns, and prayer are central elements in worship. Preaching takes about half of the service. Hymns of the day are related to the theme of the proclaimed word. Members also pray for each other with laying on of hands. As one women explained to me during group conversation, "prayer during worship is what enables people to connect with God and with each other."[93]

Fellowship is experienced in worship and doing works of ministry together. The social life and the connection between members of the church run deep. One of the things that creates such a strong connection is the culture of participatory leadership adopted by the congregation. Every member considers himself or herself as part and parcel of all activities being carried out by the congregation, from vision casting to raising funds, final implementation, and evaluation of the ministries.

Qualitative Data from Grace of God Church

I conducted a focus group conversation with ten members and a personal interview with the leading pastor of the Grace of God church, Pastor John. Participants of the focused group conversation have various responsibilities in the church.[94] Thirty-two *in vivo* codes emerged during the analysis of the focus group conversation, and twenty *in vivo* codes emerged during the analysis of personal interview with the leading pastor.[95] These *in vivo* codes were merged and grouped into twelve focused codes, which then underwent another level of abstraction, creating four axial codes (see table below).

93. See Appendix E. Participant G.
94. See Appendix E.
95. See Appendix F.

Table 4. Grace of God Church Axial and Focus Codes

Axial Codes	Focused Codes
Self-identification as a healing, praying, and reconciling fellowship of believers.	Identify themselves as a healing community. Describe themselves as a "praying community". Describe church as a reconciling fellowship of believers.
Engaged in holistic ministry with a focus on evangelism.	Emphasize holistic care for members. Engaged in public ministry Provide social and development services. Youth and children ministry Focus on evangelism, planting congregations.
Value African cultural heritage.	Value African cultural heritage. Dilemma with the relationship between some cultural elements and gospel
Exercise leadership formation and empowerment.	Leadership formation and empowerment processes Culture of shared leadership

Table 6 illustrates the relationship between axial codes and focused codes. The first axial code illustrates the self-identification of the church as a *healing, praying, and reconciling fellowship of believers*. Here, all the three terms are emphasized in how the church describes its identity. The church is a place where *healing* (physical and spiritual) and *reconciliation* (with God and others) is experienced. *Healing* and *reconciliation* are experienced when a community of believers take part in worship and fellowship while being committed in *prayer*.

The church gives priority to *serving the whole person*. The emphasis, however, is on evangelism. The public engagements of the church (development, advocacy, and so on) are meant to support evangelistic ministry of the church. Some elements of *African cultural values* provide the premises through which the congregation's self-identity, theology, and practice are shaped. *Leadership formation and empowerment* refer to the impact of the churches self-identification, its holistic engagement, and its openness to adopt *African traditional values* on emerging leaders (See figure 5 below).

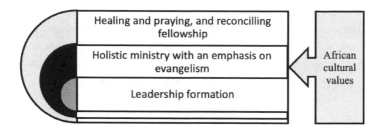

Figure 6: Axial Codes from the Grace of God Church

Figure 6 above illustrates the relationship between axial codes. The figure shows the interconnection between the self-identification of the church (*healing*, *praying*, and *reconciling fellowship*), its activity (*holistic ministry*), and the *leadership formation* praxis of the congregation. As shown in the figure, the *African cultural values* are connected to the other three axial codes (stated above). The way it is connected to other axial codes indicates that its influence in shaping the identity and activities of the church is limited or partial. The grace of God church is very critical to African cultural values in that they filter and adopt few based on their understanding of how those cultures relate to the gospel.

The primary goal of the church is realizing their own identity and how such identity can be practically expressed. For them, the church is able to provide *holistic* service when it is able to attain its true self or identity. In other words, the church's action or activities are products of its identity. *African traditional values* inform the self-understanding and praxis of the church. These values form a context in which the self-identity as well as ministries of the church are framed. *Leadership formation* and empowerment is a process that results from both the self-identification and the traditional values that form a context. From these axial codes, what we can understand about the Grace of God Church (theoretical code) is that it is a culturally informed *healing*, *praying*, and *reconciling* fellowship of believers that focuses on evangelistic ministry with other ministries (social, development, and so on) supporting and strengthening its main ministry.

A Healing, Reconciling, and Praying Fellowship

A *healing, reconciling, and praying fellowship* is one of the axial codes identified during the analysis of qualitative data collected from Grace of God Church. During group conversation, I asked the congregation's view of the church. Many talked about the church as a healing community. They used words like "reconciliation," "healing," and "fellowship" to describe their understanding of what it means to be a church.[96] When I asked how they describe their congregation, a women emphasized that "in the midst of a country where peoples' life is endangered in many ways, the congregation presents itself as a community where those troubles in life can get healing."[97] She said, "We identify our congregation as a healing community."[98] The members believe in the power of healing by prayer and the laying on of hands. They also understand that God's healing power is revealed in fellowship, the midst of a caring and loving community of people bound together by love for one another.

Some also asserted that the congregation identifies itself as a "reconciling fellowship of believers."[99] Reconciliation with God and with others (both members of the congregation and those they serve) is emphasized. For them, God's ultimate purpose as revealed in the Scriptures is reconciliation, reconciliation between the creation and God. Therefore, the healing power of God is experienced when one is reconciled with God and others.

The congregation also identifies itself as a "praying community."[100] They believe in the power of prayer and in sharing this power with each other and others in their community. Each week, they make a call for prayer at the congregation as well as in villages. Each member is expected to participate in either or both programs. As one man explained, "it is the power of prayer that has direct impact on people's faith in God and their participation in God's work within and outside their congregation."[101]

When asked what biblical stories or passages they use to describe a church, they referred to Acts 2:42–47. They said that a church is where they devote ourselves to (1) "the apostles' teaching," (2) "the fellowship, to

96. Appendix F. Participant B, C, F.

97. Appendix F. Participant G.

98. Appendix F. Participant G.

99. Appendix F. Participant A, F, H.

100. Appendix F. Participant H, I.

101. Appendix F. Participant H, I.

the breaking of bread," (3) "the prayers," (4) a place where "many wonders and signs [are] being done," (5) and where "possessions and belongings" are distributed to those in need. In short, they emphasized the church is where healing from the social, economic, political, and spiritual problems and dilemmas is experienced.[102]

Holistic Ministry

Holistic ministry is another axial code identified during the analysis of qualitative data collected from Grace of God Church. The Grace of God Church has a commitment to caring for its members' needs. Its self-identification as a healing, praying, and reconciling community has contributed to its commitment to each member as well as others. As a healing and reconciling community of faith, members are happy to extend their hospitality to visitors. Their hospitality is expressed in making people feel welcome and cared for when they come for whatever reason. Particularly during worship services, the time of fellowship after Sunday church service, and programs held in villages (Bible study and prayer), their hospitality is visible.

The congregation is actively engaged in community services. The members describe their role as a healing community holistically in such a way that it encompasses physical and spiritual healing. To provide spiritual healing, they have worship, prayer, education, counseling, and Bible study programs in which everyone is welcome to participate. For the physical healing, they are engaged in other material and non-material support through which people of the communities are served.

The congregation focuses on ways to reach out and assist the community, mainly due to its location among the many people who lack the basic necessities of life. Their community service is holistic in nature, and they provide assistance for the physical needs while also proclaiming the good news of the gospel.

They have water pump projects, educational assistance, and also other kinds of projects where they provide food and clothing. Evangelism and outreach programs are also major activities of the congregation. The congregation is engaged in planting congregations through different outreach programs. Currently, there are seven outreach areas. In all these outreach areas, the congregation is also engaged in development activities such as

102. Appendix F. Participant H, I.

water pump projects, schools, provision of food and clothing for the needy, and so on.

Leadership Formation

Leadership formation is the other axial code identified during the analysis of qualitative data collected from Grace of God Church. The Grace of God Church focuses on interpersonal relationship and community-building in teachings. In their ministry and teaching, they aspire to be a caring community that also challenges people to grow personally and spiritually. When asked how leaders are raised in their congregation, some talked about activities of communal life as a context in which leaders are raised. A woman asserted that "it is when members participate in church miniseries as a community that they create an opportunity to connect and interact. It is in such connection and interaction that we see leaders emerging. They are formed by matured members of the community as they act together."[103]

Others stated the impact of small fellowship groups organized both within the congregation as well as outside as having a major impact on the life and ministry of emerging leaders, as the pastor of the congregation had once asserted that this congregation is "the community of small groups organized in villages."[104] Such an approach helps the congregation to help each member grow in faith and have a better understanding of the Scriptures through focused small-group Bible studies and prayer programs.

In the Grace of God Church, leadership is shared. They have a lay leadership that is not dominated by other leaders, but includes younger and older generations. Women's ministry is also given proper consideration, as they take the lead in most activities, particularly in community services. The role of pastors and evangelists is to coordinate people to lead ministries within and outside the congregation.

Leaders are devoted in helping people make connections and forming networks of people leading ministries of the congregation. Such a practice enabled members to know each other in a deeper sense, and better serve each other. The community is formed and leaders emerge around being involved in doing ministry together. As they are involved in ministries together, they walk alongside each other, which in many ways helps them to connect and share each other's lives.

103. Appendix F. Participant G.
104. Pastor John, See Appendix B.

The topic of leadership formation was explored more in the personal interview with Pastor John, pastor of Grace of God Church. When I asked his understanding of a leader, Pastor John responded that "a leader is someone with a sense of vocation, vision, and mission. A leader is someone who is able to build and work in relationships. Particularly in the African context, where leadership cannot be sustained if not nurtured in relationships, a leader needs to be someone with the capability to build, nurture, and sustain relationships. A leader is someone who can observe and interpret his context to his/her followers."[105]

The follow-up question was, "what is required to be a leader?" Pastor John stated leadership in church context requires calling. Leadership is a response to calling. It also requires commitment to prayer and devotional life. Leadership is also capability to build, nurture, and sustain relationships. It requires the ability to build trust through respect (credibility), listening, and developing a culture of decision making in which he/she involves each and every individual in his/her community.[106]

When asked what members of his congregation think about the role and responsibility of a leader, Pastor John asserted that members of his congregation mainly see community-building skills as the main role of leaders. He stated, "Life here is all about community."[107] The leader has to be skilled in dealing with people, shared leadership, and have capacity to motivate others. They also expect credibility, transpArén cy, cooperativeness, and internalized self-control.

African cultural values is also another axial code which emerged during the analysis of qualitative data collected from the Grace of God Church. This axial code emerged in relation to the researcher's interest in exploring the impact of African cultural values on the self-identification and practice of the Grace of God Church. One good example is the question asked on what cultural languages or images are used to describe a leader. Pastor John stated that among the Oromo, the *ungaafa* (elders) are assumed to be wise, and are therefore trusted to be capable leaders.[108] The cultural understanding is that their wisdom is acquired from their long years of experience. The authority of *ungaafa* is built on their reputation and personal behavior. In OTR, the *ungaafa* are representatives of *Waaqa* (God), and are believed

105. Personal interview with Pastor John.
106. Pastor John.
107. Pastor John.
108. Pastor John.

to possess supernatural power that enables them to provide fertility and blessing. The leadership of *ungaafa* extends to every realm of life (spiritual, economic, and political).

The follow-up question was, "what are this congregation's contributions in the formation and empowering of leaders?" Pastor John asserted that "formation of leaders happens in two ways in two different locations. God is the one that forms and empowers leaders. But God's involvement in leaders' lives happens through spiritual activities (worship, teaching classes like confirmation and discipleship, evangelism, and others) within and outside the church where members are engaged in community services."[109]

A majority of the members spend most of their time outside the church building. For many of them, people with whom they spend most of the time are not church members. Some work for the government, some own their own businesses, and others are employees of non-governmental organizations. The congregation has unemployed members as well. Therefore, the activities in which they are engaged are mostly not connected to the congregation. But no matter where they are, they are evangelists, missionaries, and representatives before the community. God uses them to engage the world by virtue of ways which they are formed and empowered.[110]

COMPARING QUALITATIVE DATA FROM SOURCE OF LIFE, FAMILY LIFE, LOVE IN ACTION, AND GRACE OF GOD CHURCH

The main purpose of this study is to analyze the culture of the EECMY congregations and their implication in the formation and empowerment of emerging leaders. In the sections above, I have described the findings of the study for each congregations that was studied. Each of these findings are compared below to allow for proper dialogue between all four EECMY congregations.

The comparison is essential to allow for a broader discussion of the big concepts that emerged from the coding process. For this reason, I compared the axial codes and theoretical codes from both the focus group conversation and personal interview from Source of Life Church, Family Life Church, Love in Action Church, and Grace of God Church.

109. Pastor John.
110. Pastor John.

Most axial codes that emerged from the four congregations had much in common. The common axial codes identified are *holistic* (in relation to the service they provide), *African cultural values* (which informs their identity and activities), and their experience of *leadership formation*. The research findings show what all four congregations share in common in terms of their practices of the formation of emerging leaders (See figure 6 below).

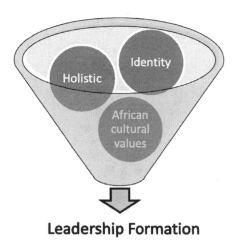

Leadership Formation

Figure 7: Common Axial Codes of the Four Congregations

Figure 7 above illustrates the research findings: It is the identity of the church (as differently identified by the studied congregations), their *holistic* engagement, and the *African cultural values* (which sets a context) that results in *leadership formation*. The ministry of the studied churches, serving the whole person (without making a distinction between the physical and the spiritual being), is interconnected with the churches' self-identification in such a way that they both inform each other (the identity informed the church's activity and vise versa). *African cultural values*, on the other hand, both set the context and also inform the church's identity and their holistic engagements.

They all share a heavy emphasis on the significance of community and relationship both in congregations as well as with the community at large. They used concepts of formation and empowerment, emphasizing the process of becoming a leader in a community. In short, group participants as well as individuals who participated in one-on-one interview shared many of the primary values and emphases that have emerged in the interview.

One difference between the three congregations is the way each of them described their identity. The Source of Life church described itself as a fellowship-oriented Bible-centered church, while the Family Life church identified itself with the *hospitality* it offers. The Love in Action church, on the other hand, described itself as a worshiping community that aspires to be a "community of disciples" while the Grace of God church identified itself as a *healing community*.

Another noticeable difference between the theoretical codes of the four congregations is the emphasis of their ministry. The Source of Life church and Love in Action church describe evangelism as part and parcel of their holistic engagement while Family Life church and Grace of God church emphasize evangelism as major part of their mission. In other words, for Source of Life church and Love in Action church, the church's mission is to be engaged in holistic ministry by valuing all kinds of ministry (physical and spiritual) as equally significant. For the Family Life church and Grace of God church, however, the spiritual aspect of ministry (evangelism) is given the priority, and other ministries are considered as supportive ministries.

SUMMARY

I have presented in this chapter the result of the research that I have described in the previous chapters. I presented the resulting focused, axial, and theoretical codes that emerged from the coding process, and showed how all of the codes are connected. Finally, I compared the responses of participants from each organization with one another to find cross-congregational similarities and differences. The result of this research are unified in their suggestion that the culture of congregations engaged in holistic ministry have direct impact on the formation and empowerment of emerging leaders. The next chapters, chapters 7 and 8, attends more fully to the implication of these results and their intersection with the theological, biblical, and theoretical lenses that were presented in chapter 3 and 4.

Chapter 7

THEOLOGICAL AND BIBLICAL REFLECTION ON THE RESEARCH FINDINGS

THIS RESEARCH HAS SOUGHT to explore the impact of congregational cultures on the formation and empowerment of emerging leaders. The study focused on four Oromo-speaking congregations of the EECMY. The research question that this research project sought to address was the following: How do cultures of congregations engaged in holistic ministry form and empower emerging leaders?

Holistic ministry is participation of the believing community in God's ongoing creative work of nurturing the whole aspect of life (physical and spiritual) without separation. The missional church participates in God's mission by serving the society and the whole creation holistically. Through holistic ministry, it empowers and transforms individuals and communities.

The EECMY articulated its understanding of development or holistic ministry for the first time in 1972 in a letter sent to the Lutheran World Federation (LWF) with the title *On the Integration between Proclamation of the Gospel and Human Development*.[1] As the title of the letter indicates, the word "integration" is at the core of the EECMY's understanding about development and the church's ministry. The letter was written as a response to westerners' dichotomy of the proclamation of the gospel and human

1. Tumsa, *Witness and Discipleship*, 95–98.

development in relation to their mission works and donations in Africa, particularly the LWF.

In the 1972 letter of the EECMY, leaders like Gudina Tumsa argued that the two dimensions of ministry (the spiritual and physical) of the congregations should be carried out together. In the EECMY letter, it is stated that "an Integral Human Development, where the spiritual and material needs are seen together, is the only right approach to development questions in [African] societies."[2] It is a one-sided development approach which either focuses on the spiritual or material needs of the society that the EECMY's letter opposed. According to the EECMY's letter, the right and sustainable development approach is the one that integrates the two in an inseparable way. This approach, according to the letter, can be considered as "a process of liberation by which individuals and societies realize their human possibilities in accordance with God's purpose."[3] This research explores if this theology is being practiced within the EECMY congregations, and if so, how it impacts the formation of leaders.

I described the qualitative data gathered from focus group conversations as well as one-one-one interviews with the leading pastors of each congregations. Finally, the qualitative data from each congregation were brought into conversation with one another. This triangulation confirmed one thing: emerging leaders are formed and empowered by cultures (as identified in the self-identification and activities of the studied congregations) of congregations engaged in holistic ministry.

In this chapter, I will describe how the results of the research intersect with the theological frames that serve as the background for the study as discussed in chapters 3 and 4. In this chapter, the results from the qualitative data are brought into conversation with the theological frames which were discussed in chapter 3 (the doctrine of the Trinity and missional leadership).

THE DOCTRINE OF TRINITY

As described in chapter 3, the doctrine of Trinity is used as one of the theological frameworks for this research. The concept of Trinity has been used in many publications to explore and describe the identity and activities of the church. The significance of the doctrine of Trinity for this research is its

2. Tumsa, *Witness and Discipleship*, 89.

3. Tumsa, *Witness and Discipleship*, 89.

practical implication for the social reality of the church. God is a relational community, and the church is the community on earth that reflects the divine life.

The main interest of this research is to explore the culture of the EEC-MY congregations engaged in holistic ministry and their impact on leadership formation. As described in previous chapters (chapters 5 and 6), the study of the culture of congregation (as suggested by Ammerman) should focus on the identity and activities of the congregations.[4] The concept of Trinity also provide a significant theological grounding for understanding both the identity and activities of the studied congregations and the process of leadership formation.[5]

As Van Gelder emphasizes, the identity and activity of congregations is the Trinitarian notion of God. This means our identity as well as activity are both informed and formed by how we understand the Triune God's ongoing involvement in our world. Our activity is to *do* with our identity, what *we are* as a congregation.[6] We engage each other and the world missionaly because the Triune God is a missionary God.

Figure 8 below demonstrates how the studied congregations describe their identity. As the figure indicates, the concept of the Trinity informs the congregations' self-defined identities or how the congregations understand their identity in relation to God's mission. These self-identifications of the congregations also have an impact or influence on how they understand their ministry or activities in God's mission.

4. Ammerman, *Studying Congregations.*

5. This research does not attempt to explore the congregations' understanding of the Trinity. It opened the door for participants to reflect on their ministry in the context of a Trinitarian framework. However, all the studied congregations were silent about it. Therefore, the Trinitarian framework in this research is limited to its use as theological foundation to explore the identity and activity of the studied congregations.

6. Van Gelder, *Essence of the Church,* 128, 157.

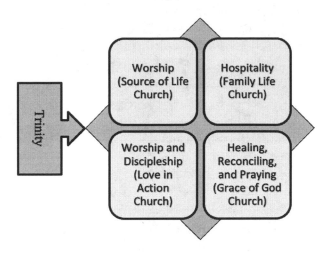

Figure 8: Self-Identification of the Studied Congregations

One of the most striking similarities between the four EECMY congregations is that the concept of community is at the core of their identity (see figure 8), activity, and leadership praxis. What should be emphasized is that they all use the term "of God" at the end of their self-description (e.g. worshiping community of God), which shows that God's mission is at the center of their self-identification. The concept of community (in the studied congregations) is adopted from African tradition and their understanding of church as community of believers. Members of all four congregations highlight the importance of community (or relationship) in their worship life, public ministry, and so on.

The Source of Life Church describes its communal identity as a fellowship-focused *worshiping* family of God. Fellowship with each other and the larger community is at the core of this congregation's identity. Family Life Church identifies itself as a community of God offering hospitality, *manaa ummaata*. With a focus on providing hospitality to the community it serves, it defines itself as a community of believers ready to embrace all and engage the larger community with the gospel of Jesus Christ.

Love in Action Church identifies itself as a worshiping community of God, *waaqeffana*, focused on discipleship making. For this church, both worship and discipleship making is at the heart of its ministry. To be a community for this church is to nurture each other through worship and other ministries that result in the formation of members to be Christ's true disciples. As disciples of Christ, they are engaged in serving the community both spiritually and physically. For Grace of God Church, the church is a healing community of God. For the church to be a healing community, it needs to engage itself in the work of the Triune God through connecting with each other and the community at large.

The results of the studied congregations also shows that formation happens in a context where there exist a relationship, and where individuals interact with their fellow brothers and sisters in Christ, with others, and with God. All that we see in figure 8 (the congregation's self-identity) is put into practice in a context where there exists such relationship. The studied congregations worship, offer hospitality, form a community of disciples, and create a healing, reconciling, and praying community through adopting a culture of interrelationship.

A quote from Pastor Matthew of the Source of Life Church captures this very well: "[In our congregation] formation and empowerment happen mainly in a context where believers are in fellowship with God and with each other."[7] In a focus group conversation at Grace of God Church, a woman also indicated that the congregation presents itself as a healing and reconciling community of believers where the fractured communities can receive God's restoration, and those who participate in this ministry (where the Triune God restores the life of others) experience transformation in their own life.[8]

It is the concept of the Trinity that helps us understand the dynamics of such interrelationship. It also offers us a lens into exploring the relationship between humans and humans' relationship with God and creation. The church and its ministry is defined within this dynamic of relationships because its main existence is founded on its mission—which is to take part in the ongoing creative work of the Triune God. As LaCugna noted, "The Trinity is ultimately about God's life with us and our life with each other [and with the whole of creation]."[9]

It is in this relationship that the Triune God shares His perichoretic life with us in the Eucharist, and that is when our life is formed into the likeness of Christ. The life of the Triune God is shared within the context of the congregations where the gospel is preached and sacraments are administered. In this way, congregations become spiritual nurseries where Christ forms

7. Personal Interview with Pastor Matthew.
8. Group conversation at Grace of God church, participant G.
9. LaCugna, God for Us, 1.

and empowers the lives of members for service in the congregation and society. When we talk about the formation and empowerment of emerging leaders, we are referring to how the Triune God shares His perichoretic life through the sacrament of the Eucharist, and how God forms and empowers leaders through the Word to live out the social implications of God's perichoretic life in all spheres of life.

Members are formed not only through activities that take place within the four walls of the congregation (such as teachings, worship, Bible study fellowships, and so on), but also through being practically engaged in public ministries. As Luther indicated in *The Bondage of the Will*, the Triune God "does not work in us without us, because he has created and preserved us that he might work in us and we might cooperate with him, whether outside his kingdom through his general omnipotence or inside his Kingdom by the special virtue of his Spirit."[10] This means God works in us (or continues to form and empower us) as we engage or "cooperate" in His work.

As Van Gelder also emphasized, the church is "a community of mutual participation in God's own life and the life of the world—a participation characterized by openness to others."[11] This is reflected in Jesus' prayer found in John 17:21–23: "As you, Father, are in me and I am in you, may they also be in us, so that the world may believe that you have sent me." As a women emphasized during Group Conversation, "it is when [the EECMY congregation] members participate in church ministries as a community" that an opportunity is created to connect and interact with God, each other, and others. It is within this connection that the Triune God is experienced, and emerging leaders are formed.

MISSIONAL CHURCH

As described in the third chapter, what the missional church conversation introduced was the Trinitarian reconceptualization of Christian mission. It resulted in a shift from understanding mission as a mere activity of the church to mission as rooted in God's purpose to restore the creation. The church is called to participate in this mission as part and parcel of the body of Christ.[12]

10. Luther, *Bondage of the Will*, 243.

11. Van Gelder and Zscheile, *Missional Church in Perspective*, 107.

12. Simpson, "No Trinity, No Mission."; Van Gelder and Zscheile, *Missional Church in Perspective*.

According to Roxburgh and Romanuk, the missional church can be understood as the gathering of "the people of God, called to be *formed* into a unique social community whose life together is the sign, witness, and foretaste of what God is doing in and for all of creation."[13] This means there are three primary focuses or characteristics of missional churches: (1) *Life together* (community), (2) *Witness*: engaging the public by participating in the ongoing work of the Triune God, and (3) *Spiritual formation* and *empowerment* of each member, in which members are enabled for such ministry.

This is similar to what Simpson identifies as the two roles of missional churches in their community: "the moral formation of their members" within the church and the church serving as "a meeting place of private and public life."[14] What Roxburgh and Romanuk identify under *spiritual formation* is what Simpson describes as "moral formation of members" because with the spiritual formation comes moral formation. The *witness* or public engagement of the church is described by Simpson as the public life of the church. *Life together* is the life of Christians as disciples of Christ, both forming their community and engaging the public.

Figure 9: Dimensions of Missional Church

13. Roxburgh and Romanuk, *Missional Leader*, 14. Emphasis mine.
14. Simpson, "Civil Society and Congregations," 426.

Figure 9 above illustrates the three dimensions of a missional church described by Roxburgh and Romanuk. First is *life together*. The missional church as a community of believers is *life together*—together with each other as brothers and sisters in Christ and with the Triune God in their midst. It is this togetherness that defines their identity and shapes their ministry. What is mostly ignored in the missional church conversation is that togetherness also extends what Simpson describes as the church's commitment as "public moral companions." In other words, the church as a community (*life together*) should "exist as a meeting place of private and public life."[15]

This leads us to the second dimension of the missional church, the church as a *witness*. The witness of the missional church is related to or founded on its *life together*. The church's *witness* is its public ministry. The missional churches become witnesses by engaging in the ongoing creative work of the Triune God through multiple kinds of ministries. The third dimension is *spiritual formation*. In *Missional Church*, the concept of spiritual formation or cultivating the Christian community was emphasized (see chapters 6 and 7) as one of the main foci of missional church conversation.[16] The missonal church forms and empowers people for God's mission in the world. The Triune God is the one that calls, forms (empowers), and sends God's people to engage the world.

The main interest of this research is to explore the leadership formation process in the EECMY congregations. The finding of the study shows that the *life together* (identity) and *witness* (holistic ministry) of the congregations have direct impact on the formation of missional leaders. With all the three dimensions of missional church displayed, the studied EECMY congregations demonstrate what it means to be a missional church in the African context.

To explore how these three dimensions of the missional church are displayed in the life and ministry of the four studied congregations, I will focus on the theoretical codes identified in the previous chapter. The theoretical code identified for the Source of Life Church "is that its main value or objective is to be a Bible-centered worshiping *community* of believers that works for the *spiritual development* of its members (leadership formation

---

15. Simpson, "Civil Society," 426

16. In this book, formation of the missional church is described as the role of missional leaders. In fact, "missional leadership: equipping God's people for mission" was the title of chapter 7.

and empowerment) and *serving others holistically*."[17] This church has its life together (the community), emphasizes the significance of spiritual formation, and values its witness to the public (holistic ministry).

When it comes to the theoretical code identified for the Family Life Church, "leaders are *formed* and *empowered* in the context where the church defines its identity as a church that *offers hospitality* and is engaged in culturally informed practices of *holistic ministry* with an emphasis on evangelism."[18] The Love in Action Church is also a "culturally informed faith-based worshiping *community* of *disciples* engaged in *serving* the whole person."[19] Finally, the Grace of God Church identifies itself as "a culturally informed healing, praying, and reconciling *fellowship* of believers that focuses on evangelistic *ministry* with other ministries (social, development, and so on) supporting and *strengthening* its main ministry."[20]

What this research contributes to the missional church conversation is related to how we understand the process of leadership formation. As the research findings show, leadership formation does not happen only within the interaction of a leader and followers. Leadership formation is more integrated in that it also involves interaction among members (*life together*) and our encounter with others (*witness*). In other words, leadership formation of members does not happen only within the four walls of the church. It also happens when they encounter strangers (neighbors). In other words, as Van Gelder rightly articulates, believers "are formed spiritually as faithful disciples through immersion not only in a vibrant, participating community where we learn from mature mentors in the faith, but also through coming to recognize the signs of the Triune God's movement in the lives of our neighbors and our world."[21]

Missional Leadership

As described in chapter 3, in the missional church conversation, the definition of missional leadership mainly focuses on "influence," the influence of a leader on their followers. Such an understanding of leadership echoes leadership theories developed in the western individualistic culture where

17. For more details, see page 198.
18. For more details, see 215.
19. For more details, see 229–30.
20. For more detail, see 245.
21. Van Gelder and Zscheile, *Missional Church*, 151.

"I am" is more emphasized than "we are."[22] Missional leadership, however, is not about a leader, but about a relationship.

As Doornenbal also emphasized, missional leadership is "the conversational process of envisioning, cultural and *spiritual formation*, and structuring within a Christian community that enables individual participants, groups, and the *community* as a whole to respond to challenging situations and *engage in transformative* changes that are necessary to become, or remain, oriented to God's mission in the local context."[23] The "conversational process" happens in a relationship, and God is at the center of this conversation and is the one who works within the community to form and empower believers for His mission. Just as Leith Anderson also described, leadership should not be merely about leaders, but "about a matrix of followers, circumstances, power, and history."[24] This understanding about leadership is related to what Warren Bennis describes as leadership in the new era—leadership "as an organizational capability and not an individual characteristic that a few in individuals at the top of the organization have."[25]

The emphasis of missional leadership is equipping "saints for the work of ministry, for building up the body of Christ," and this is what we refer to as formation and empowerment of believers for ministry (Eph 4:11–12). Saints are equipped in the missional church where the Word is preached and sacraments are administered. Equipping saints is the work of God, and that is why it is emphasized that "leadership formation must be asked only in terms of what God is doing in forming the social community known as ecclesia."[26] In the missional church, all of Christ's is equipped so that they can function in a way that they all contribute to building the whole body by equipping each other as a community.

The findings of this research also suggests that leadership (in the African context) is more about relationship in a community and about

22. For Alan Hirsch, for example, leadership should be understood as "a field that shaped behaviors." See Hirsch, *Forgotten Ways*, 152. Terri Elton also focuses largely on leaders. For her, missional leadership "includes persons who understand their calling as disciples of Jesus Christ, see themselves as equipped by God with certain gifts, and believe that they are empowered by the Spirit to engage the world by participating in the creative and redemptive mission of God." See Elton, "Charactoristics of Congregations," 178. See also Doornenbal, *Crossroads*, 357.

23. Doornenbal, *Crossroads*, 200. Emphasis mine.

24. Anderson, *Leadership That Works*, 44.

25. Bennis, "Leading from the Grass Roots," 24.

26. Roxburgh and Romanuk, *Missional Leader*, 118.

formation and empowerment of leaders in a context where life in community is experienced. In other words, missional leadership is best understood as an aspect of a community rather than as a possession of the leader—"a communal capacity and a communal achievement."[27] Such an understanding about leadership shifts the focus from a leader-centered approach to a shared leadership exercised in a Christian community. Furthermore, missional leadership involves involvement of the Christian community in public ministry. Missional leaders are also formed in their encounter with the "other" and God's creation as a whole—and this is what is described as *integrated missional leadership formation* (see figure 1 in chapter 1).

How do the studied congregations of the EECMY understand missional leadership? Pastor Matthew, the pastor of the Source of Life church describes eldership in relationship terms. He argues that a leader's role is inspiring members of the congregation to achieve their goal through the established relationship between the leader and members. By "achieving a goal," he means helping members to a point where they are able to share their God-given talents with each other and others.[28] For Pastor Mark (Family Life church), a leader is "someone who nurtures his followers to grow in relationship"[29] For Pastor Luke, a leader is "someone committed to shared leadership."[30]For Pastor John, a leader is someone who is able to build and work in relationships.[31] Based on how pastors of the studied congregations understand leadership, we can conclude that there are two things that are common to all: that leadership is about relationship, and that this relationship involves formation and empowerment of leaders.

The studied congregations use different cultural languages to describe leadership which demonstrates their understanding about missional leadership. According to Pastor Matthew of the Source of Life church, the Oromo word *Lubaa* (traditional Oromo name for a religious leader) is used to describe a leader as responsible in all realms of life, not only the spiritual.[32] This word is mainly used for ordained ministers of the Word and

27. Expression borrowed from Drath, *Deep Blue See*, xvi.

28. See Personal Interview with Pastor Matthew, Pastor of Source of Life Church, pages 205–9.

29. See Personal Interview with Pastor Mark, Family Life Church, pages 222–26.

30. See Personal Interview with Pastor Luke, Love in Action Church, pages 238–40.

31. See Personal Interview with Pastor John, Grace of God Church, pages 249–52.

32. See Personal Interview with Pastor Matthew, Pastor of Source of Life Church, page 205.

Sacrament. The plural term *Luboota* is used to refer to priesthood of all believers—that all believers share the role of leadership. There is activity in the congregation in which the *Luboota* are not involved except administering sacraments.

For Pastor Mark, the term *raaga* or *waa argaa* (seer) gives more meaning to how leaders are understood culturally. The word *raaga* or *waa argaa* refers to a leader who envisions the future or a visionary leader.[33] According to Pastor John, the term *ungaafa* (elders) is used to denote the significance of wisdom in leadership. Both pastors also agree that envisioning or planning and all activities of the congregation (which requires shared wisdom) happen in a shared leadership which requires a strong relationship between all members, and God is at the center of this relationship.

When we move to how emerging leaders are formed and empowered by the culture of the studied congregations, the results of this research indicate that the culture of shared leadership adopted by all the studied congregations have a major contribution in the life and ministry of emerging leaders. Most activities of these congregations are led by lay ministers. As some members from Family Life Church emphasized, the tradition of shared leadership adopted by the EECMY congregations created an opportunity for leaders to emerge.[34] According to Pastor Matthew, "the EECMY's tradition of giving each believer the opportunity to serve regardless of his/her age and ministerial position is what enables leaders to emerge, and to grow in service."[35] It is this culture of shared leadership that created opportunity for members to be formed through connecting with each other and others outside their circle. Pastors in these congregation simply facilitate and help all members exercise their gifts in sharing their God-given talents with the wider society. Pastors and evangelists describe their vocation as direction-setting or guiding the congregation towards such practice.

The difference, however, is that not all of the studied congregation of the EECMY experience integrated leadership formation (which is described in figure 10 below). Though they all experience the impact of ministries taking place within the four walls of the church and through reaching out to others for evangelism, it is only the two congregations (the Source of Life

33. See Personal Interview with Pastor Mark, Pastor of Family Life Church, on page 223.

34. Family Life church group conversation, participant A, B, G, I, J.

35. Pastor Matthew, personal interview, page 205.

Church and Love in Action Church) that experience leadership formation through encountering "others" in their advocacy ministry.

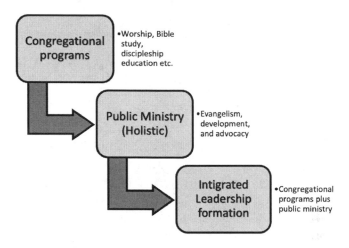

Figure 10: Integrated Leadership Formation Praxis in EECMY Congregations

Figure 10 above shows that integrated leadership formation happens when congregations are engaged in holistic ministry without dichotomizing the spiritual and physical services. In other words, integrated leadership formation happens in congregations that adopt the culture of service to the whole person (engaging the spiritual, social, economic, and political life of the society they serve). The finding of this research, however, show that only two congregations of the EECMY (Source of Life Church and Love in Action Church) have adopted this culture. In these two congregations, merging leaders are formed and empowered through the spiritual and social activities that take place both in the congregations and outside their walls.

All four congregations are similar in their engagement in their spiritual services and evangelism work. The spiritual services conducted in all four congregations include women's programs, children and youth programs, counselling, Bible study programs, diaconal programs (intended to serve needy members), prayer services (in the church and villages), worship services, and so on. Members are formed and empowered by participating in these ministries from their childhood to adulthood. More importantly, these congregations are focused on discipleship making—education programs designed to help members matured in their faith. Through these programs, they challenge members to engage in ministries both within the church and outside. As a woman from Love in Action Church noted, the education programs are mainly planned and conducted with the aim of "enriching children, youth, and adults to emerge as leaders and serve each other and the community with better preparedness and knowledge."[36]

The focus of the congregations on teaching the Word during worship, teaching ministries, and village Bible study programs has a major impact on shaping the life and ministry of members. The Source of Life Church refers to themselves as "Bible believing members" use statements such as "our faith and praxis is founded on Bible, " and "we are Bible-centered worshiping community" to show the place of Scripture in how they identify themselves and their ministry.[37] According to Pastor Mark, Bible study programs (both within the congregation and in the villages) provide a very strong foundation for the formation and spiritual enrichment of members.[38] When it comes to Love in Action Church, they indicated that the Lutheran understanding of the church as a place where the Word of God is preached according to the "apostles' teaching" and sacraments administered as basis for their emphasis on the teaching of the Word.[39] Members of the Grace of God Church also indicates that the Bible study and educational programs focused on nurturing the spiritual life of members have major impact in forming and empowering emerging leaders.[40]

This shows that one of the dimensions of a missional church which has a major impact on the life and ministry of members is the study of the Word of God. As Luther states, the study of the Word has a significant impact on a believers' lives and ministry because "the soul of the one who clings to the Word in true faith is so entirely united with it that all the virtues of the word becomes virtues of the soul also."[41] As Luther argues, Christ is the Word of God that is addressed to human beings as *extra nos* (outside of us), and a Word that unites humanity with the Triune God through faith. When the human soul is addressed by this Word, it is united with the Triune God in

36. Group Conversation at Love in Action church, Participant F.

37. For more detail, see 199.

38. For more detail, see 224.

39. See 231.

40. See 249.

41. Luther, "Freedom of a Christian," 24.

faith. This Word also evokes a transformation and leads to the experience of faith formation and empowerment from within.[42]

Outside the church, these EECMY congregations are active in engaging the community, and it is this engagement that also creates an environment (in addition to the congregational context)[43] for emerging leaders to be formed and empowered. There are two ways in which the studied congregations are involved in the community. First, they simply take part in social events such as weddings, funerals, and other social activities (all studied congregations are similar in this). By being involved in these social events, they show their solidarity and willingness to share the joys and sorrows in their community. According to Pastor Mark, it is such interaction of congregation members with others that results in transformative experience of emerging leaders.[44] Second, limited to the Source of Life Church and Love in Action Church as described above, they provide holistic services to their community. (This will be explained more in the section below under holistic ministry).

LUKE AND ACTS: HOLISTIC MINISTRY AND LEADERSHIP FORMATION

As described in chapter 3, the gospel of Luke and the book of Acts provides us with a biblical framework through which we can understand the concept of holistic ministry and leadership from a biblical perspective. Luke mainly deals with the life and ministry of Jesus and through that, he describes his holistic approach to ministry and how his disciples and other followers were formed and empowered as a result. He demonstrates how the Triune God sent His only son as a holistic being not only to share the good news, but to also share his holistic being and meet the social, economic, and political needs of the people we serve.

This brings us to the understanding that God's mission is holistic, and that the church is invited to be part of this mission. In Luke-Acts, it is within such an understanding of God's mission that the concept of formation is described. The disciples were formed and empowered to be missional leaders as they engaged the teaching of Jesus and the public. They were formed and were also the means for others to be formed in Christ's likeness.

42. Luther, "Freedom of a Christian," 24.

43. Or activities that take place within the four walls of the church.

44. Personal interview with Pastor Mark, 222–26.

As the study shows, emerging leaders are formed and empowered in relationships with each other and others outside their circle. They empower each other so that each member are able to be engaged in ministry. Being in relationship or in community is vital for these congregations. In the Gospel of Luke, we find Jesus calling and taking time with twelve disciples to form and empower them in their ministries to the world. Jesus did not engage his disciples on a one-to-one basis, but rather nurtured their faith as a community. For him, it was vital for them to be in fellowship with him as well as with each other. In the Book of Acts, these disciples followed Jesus's example and formed communities to empower ministries. In fact, as Guder emphasize, "the Scriptures collective purpose was the continuing formation of already-missional communities for faithful and obedient witness."[45]

Furthermore, the study also shows that engaging others in public space (as we see in Source of Life Church and Love in Action Church) is vital for leadership formation. In fact, the integrated formation of emerging leaders happens between in-house (congregational) ministries and holistic public engagement of the congregations. This is also what we observe in the life and ministry of Jesus. Jesus was holistic in his ministry. He came to this world to restore his people through the power of the Holy Spirit (Luke 4:16–21). This restoration is to be manifested in the lives of the poor and the oppressed as compassion and justice prevail. Jesus did not only engage the disciples with words-of-mouth. Christ, God's gift to humanity, came as a servant and shared his own self, laying down his life for all.

When it comes to the studied congregations, the findings of the research show that the ministry of the four EECMY congregations focus on three areas: *evangelism*, *development*, and *advocacy*. *Evangelism* is the major activity of the four congregations, with more budget assigned to it than all other ministries. They all have outreach programs through which they plant new congregations.[46] They are all also involved in different *development* activities. Development programs are run both within the congregations (targeting the needy members) and among the community.[47]

---

45. Guder, *Called to Witness*, 66.

46. See figure 11.

47. See figure 11. The development activities include building of community school, digging well projects, women's empowerment projects, child sponsorship programs, donkey projects, small-scale business training, capacity building projects, and so on. Members participate in envisioning these projects, allocating fund, and running the programs.

When it comes to *advocacy*, all the studied congregations participate in awareness-raising programs with other congregations of the EECMY on health, domestic violence, and so on. They also implement the motto of Peace Office, an office of the EECMY established to coordinate the work of advocacy at the national level, at the local level.[48] The difference between them, however, is on their emphasis. Family Life Church and Grace of God Church emphasize evangelism over development and advocacy while the Source of Life Church and Love in Action Church consider all ministries as integral (all directed towards fulfilling God's mission in their society (see figure 11 below).

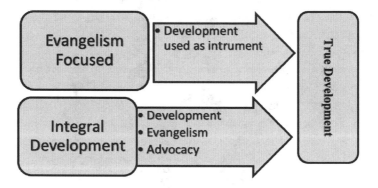

Figure 11: Ministry Emphasis of the Studied Congregations

Figure 11 above shows noticeable difference between the theoretical codes of the four congregations, mainly in the emphasis of their ministry. As the figure indicates, in the four studied congregations of the EECMY, there are two different approaches to ministry. When the Source of Life Church and Love in Action Church follow the integral approach where evangelism is considered as part and parcel of their holistic engagement, the other two, the Family Life Church and Grace of God Church emphasize evangelism as a major part of their mission.

As the research shows, only two of the four studied congrega-tions (Source of Life Church and Love in Action Church) are engaged in

48. See figure 11. The issue of advocacy is addressed under the supervision of the department of Peace Office at the national level of the EECMY. One area in which this office works actively with and through the congregations on discrimination of women and harmful traditional practices such as female genital mutilation.

advocacy. These two congregations advocate against the multifaceted forms of injustice that condemn many persons to hunger, disease, unemployment, ignorance, displacement, violent deaths, developmental stagnation, and so on. This means, as postcolonial theorists posit, they have developed a critical stand point against any form of oppression or colonialist views. The liberating culture of these two congregations is inspirational not only for the congregations alike, but also for the larger public in fighting dehumanizing structures, and in the struggling for social change and justice. Their theology and actions (the culture they developed), therefore, can only be understood and described in a context where one is able to understand this reality—the reality of oppressive systems within which these congregations carry out their activities and how they respond to it.

These two approaches to ministry demonstrate the congregations' understanding about ministry. For the one that focuses on evangelism over other ministries, the Great Commission in Matthew 28 is emphasized and interpreted as having only a spiritual meaning, that God's mission is merely concerned with "saving the lost souls." Other ministries, such as development and advocacy, are considered as non-essential for salvation, and are therefore considered secondary or supportive ministries. Those that follow an integrated approach to ministry interpret the Scripture from various dimensions and considers God's mission as concerned with all aspects of human life.

The culture adopted by two of the other studied congregations (Family Life Church and Grace of God Church), which focus on evangelism and neglect the public ministry of the church, contradicts what we see in the ministry of Jesus. A closer look at the Gospel of Luke and the Book of Acts leads to the understanding that true evangelism is contrary to what the two congregations narrowly identified as "saving the lost souls" in that it includes serving the whole man, the physical and the spiritual. At the same time, it is good to take note that using charitable works as a means for a "soul saving" strategy among the needy is unbiblical for it contradicts the gospel of Jesus Christ. As Luther emphasized, a Christian is formed into Christ's likeness when he "empt[ies] himself [and] take[s] upon himself the form of a servant to serve, help, and in every way deal with *his neighbor* as he sees that God through Christ has dealt and still deals with him."[49]

The public ministry of the four EECMY congregations are diverse. The Source of Life Church focuses on sanitation and training the youth on

---

49. Luther, "Freedom of a Christian," 366. Emphasis mine.

how to be effective entrepreneurs. The idea behind the training for entrepreneurship is ensuring sustainable development through equipping the society in economic self-support and for self-reliance. This church is also active in advocating for justice and human rights, particularly on issues related to domestic violence against women and children. On the other hand, the Family Life Church is actively involved in education, and they run projects like women's empowerment, wells, counselling, and child sponsorship. However, advocacy is not part of this church's public ministry.

The Love in Action Church is involved in activities such as HIV projects, health ministries through opening clinics, water projects, small-scale business training and capacity building projects, and educational support projects (particularly for orphaned children). This church is also active in advocacy, particularly on issues related to achieving equality between genders and people of different ethnic groups. The Grace of God Church is also actively engaged in supporting the society through water pump projects, and educational, food, and clothing assistance. This church, however, is not involved in advocacy.

In addition to the above, two congregations, Source of Life Church and Love in Action Church, through their activity in advocacy projects, address the following two central capabilities: Bodily integrity and control over one's environment.[50] None of the four studied congregations are active in addressing the following two central capabilities: other species and play.[51]

---

50. Luther, "Freedom of a Christian," 366. For Nussbaum, "bodily integrity" refers to "being able to move freely from place to place; to be secure against violation" and "control over one's environment" refers to "being able to participate effectively in political choices that govern one's life." See Nussbaum, *Creating Capabilities*, 34.

51. For Nussbaum, "other species" refers to "being able to live with concern for and in relation to animals, plants, and the world of nature" and "play" refers to "being able to laugh, to play, to enjoy recreational activities." See Nussbaum, *Creating Capabilities*, 34.

Chapter 8

THEORETICAL REFLECTIONS ON THE RESEARCH FINDINGS

FIRST, A BRIEF SUMMARY of the context within which the EECMY congregations function is presented.[1] Next, we will engage in conversation with theoretical concepts that inform the research: theory of culture and theory of leadership. Finally, I will present the significance of the study, limitations, and suggestions for future research.

UNDERSTANDING THE CONTEXT

As described in chapter 2, religion plays a vital role in Ethiopian society. Christianity, Islam, Judaism, and Traditional Religions have all contributed to shaping cultural norms and identities of various communities in Ethiopia. Among these religions, Christianity was the first to be welcomed when introduced to the Axumite kingdom of Ethiopia in the fourth century C.E. It was first introduced to the royal court and from there gradually infiltrated into the life of the common people. From its beginning to the coming of the socialist government in 1974, Ethiopian Orthodox Christianity was a state religion. Throughout the centuries, this church functioned within a "Christendom" model. As Paul Balisky has rightly noted, leaders of this church "viewed all of Ethiopia, whether pagan or Muslim, as their domain."[2]

1. For detail, see Chapter 2.
2. Balisky, "Ethiopian Church and Mission," 226.

For centuries, Islam, Traditional Religions, and other forms of Christianity (Catholicism and Evangelicalism) were considered threats to Ethiopian ideology, and were therefore under severe persecution. This mentality reached its tragic nadir when the socialist government banned all religions in 1974. With the declaration of the freedom of religion following the fall of the socialist government in 1991, this policy came to an end. A study about Christianity (or any other religion) in Ethiopia, therefore, needs to seriously consider the social, economic, and political makeup of the country.

The EECMY, which is the focus of this research, is a church with a history of over a hundred years of service. Its history starts with the endeavor of the first Lutheran missionary to Ethiopia, Peter Heyling (1607–1652).[3] It was Heyling who paved the way for the missionary endeavors that took place in the nineteenth and twentieth centuries. The most effective of these efforts was the arrival of Swedish missionaries in 1868 and their subsequent effort to evangelize the Oromo through the creation and training of indigenous missionaries.[4] These indigenous missionaries were liberated Oromo slaves and Eritrean priests. They were the first converts to the evangelical faith, and later became pioneer missionaries who translated the Scriptures into Oromo, planted schools, and preached the good news of Jesus Christ to the marginalized and oppressed communities. They preached to a people who had been deprived of social, cultural, economic, and political rights and had been reduced to second-class status within the Ethiopian empire. Their places of preaching became the foundation upon which the EECMY was instituted one hundred and twenty years ago.

Since then, the EECMY has been providing holistic service to the Ethiopian community. When the country was facing economic, social, and political problems that endangered the livelihood of the people in the last one hundred and twenty years, the EECMY stood along with them, prayed for them, and provided spiritual and humanitarian services. More importantly, in 1972, the EECMY adopted a position with regard to holistic ministry which is clearly specified in a document addressed to the Lutheran World Federation (LWF) entitled "On the Interrelation between the Proclamation of the Gospel and Human Development."[5] This research explores how emerging leaders are being formed and empowered by the cultures of the EECMY congregations that have adopted this position.

3. Arén, *Evangelical Pioneers in Ethiopia*, 37.

4. Arén, *Evangelical Pioneers in Ethiopia*, 236, 409.

5. Tumsa, *Witness and Discipleship*.

Limiting the scope of research to the Oromo-speaking congregations of the EECMY in and around Addis Ababa, the capital city of Ethiopia, this study has identified how the culture of congregational ministries impacts emerging leaders (see chapter 6). Below, what has been identified will be analyzed using theological and theoretical frameworks which were described in chapters 3 and 4 respectively.

THEORY OF CULTURE

The emphasis of this research is on exploring how emerging leaders are formed and empowered by cultures of the EECMY congregations that are engaged in holistic ministry. In the fourth chapter, I have described a theory of culture as a theoretical framework that has significant contributions for analyzing cultures of congregations. Geertz's work on theory of culture is essential for this research, for it helps us understand and explore cultures from within the real life of the studied community. More importantly, it helps us interpret the cultures of the studied congregations as insiders.[6]

As a review, based on Max Weber's description of man as "an animal suspended in webs of significance he himself has spun," Geertz reiterates that "culture is those webs, and the analysis of it [is] therefore not an experimental science in search of law but an interpretive one is search of meaning."[7] For Geertz, all actions and ritual practices (including the objects, artifacts, and so on) are parts of this web of significance that constitutes reality. The work of an interpreter is to observe and/or read the symbols that are contained in local human experience.

According to Geertz, symbols are "tangible formulations of notions, abstractions from experience fixed in perceptible forms, concrete embodiments of ideas, attitude, judgment, longings, or beliefs."[8] Congregations also display these symbols, and are therefore like texts available for interpretation. As Ramsay notes, one can identity symbols in the congregations as a way of exploring their culture by focusing on how they "unconsciously develop or evolve their own certain ways of behaving toward one another

---

6. Cultural anthropology, like ethnography, observes people from their own point of view. See Schwandt, *Qualitative Inquiry*, 101. Creswell, *Research Design*, 200.

7. Geertz, *Interpretation of Cultures*, 3.

8. Geertz, "Religion as a Cultural System," 644.

and those outside their membership [and how] they evolve a distinct identity that is carried in the language they use and the stories they tell."[9]

Roxburgh and Romanuk argue that identification of congregational culture should include the following five elements: "(1) how it views itself in relationship to the community, (2) the values that shape how it does things, (3) expectations of one another and of its leaders, (4) unspoken codes about why it exists and who it serves, how it reads Scripture, and (5) how it forms a community."[10] These five elements are symbols which Geertz describe as texts that contain meaning, and are foundational for interpreting the culture of congregations.

The first element is how a congregation *views itself in relationship to the community*. The research finding shows that all the studied congregations define their own identity based on how they understand their responsibility to each other and to the wider community. When we analyze the Source of Life Church, fellowship with each other and the larger community is at the core of this congregation's identity. Family Life Church, on the other hand, identifies itself as *manaa ummaata*, a house for the community. It describes itself in terms of hospitality that it offers to the community at large. For Love in Action Church, worship and discipleship making is at the heart of its ministry. The congregation understands itself in terms of its responsibility to nurture each other and the whole community through holistic ministry. Grace of God Church views itself through its responsibility to serve others as a healing community. For the church to be healing, it needs to engage itself in the work of the Triune God through connecting with each other and the community at large.

This leads us to the second element, *the values that shape how the congregation does things*. The findings of the research show that the congregation's identity and activities are shaped by values derived from their faith (Scriptures) and the African cultural traditions. There are two common values that shaped the ministry of the congregations: their self-identification as a community and their understanding of ministry as holistic. All studied congregations identify themselves as a community. Their understanding of church as a community is founded on both the Scripture (church as a body of Christ) and African values of communal life. When it comes to

9. Ramsay, "Congregation as a Culture," 38.

10. Roxburgh and Romanuk, *Missional Leader*, 63. For Penny Becker, interpretation of congregational culture should focus on identifying a "local understanding of identity and mission that can be understood analytically as bundles of core tasks and legitimate ways of doing things." Becker, *Congregations in Conflict*, 7.

the things they do together as a congregation, holistic ministry, it is shaped by how they understand the Scriptures (comprehensive understanding of God's engagement in our world) and the African philosophical view of man (as both physical and spiritual).

The third element is the congregations' *expectations of one another and of their leaders*. The findings of the research show that the studied congregations experience communal leadership. What members expect from ordained ministers and elders of the church is to facilitate and coordinate activities of the church which are basically carried out by lay ministers. Lay ministers are involved in envisioning as well as executing the plans with the leaders. Adopting this culture, a culture where all members act responsibly toward one another and others, is what creates conducive environment within which emerging leaders are formed and empowered.

The fourth element is *unspoken codes about why congregations exist and who they serves, and how they read Scripture*. The studied congregations' *unspoken codes* are what we simply observe or read in the congregation without anyone feeling the need to explain them. As the study shows, this *unspoken code* is Oromo cultural identity, which is displayed in the worship, communication, and dressing style of the studied congregations. This *unspoken* identity differentiates them from other congregations which are multi-cultural, and leads to their *unspoken* main target in service—the Oromo people. Though the intention to serve one's own community is commendable, the problem that such monolithic congregations face is that their service and their communicative capacity is limited. The Oromo cultural values or worldviews also shape how members interact with each other and how they read and interpret Scriptures.

The fifth element is *how the congregations form a community*. The research finding shows that the studied congregations experience leadership formation (within the church as well as in the community) in two ways: in the relationship between members and others within the four walls of the church, and how member's interact with the wider community (their engagement in holistic ministry). The congregations serve each other both spiritually (through worship, education, and so on) and physically through providing the needy with material and financial support. The focus of congregations in serving both the spiritual and physical aspects of life is what leads to integrated formation experience.

LEADERSHIP THEORY

The main emphasis of this research is to explore the formation and empowering of emerging leaders in Ethiopian context. The theory of transformational leadership (described in chapter 4) provides us with an adequate framework through which we can explore the leadership praxis of the EECMY congregations. Transformational leadership as articulated by James M. Burns is a people-centered inspirational approach "that emphasizes the importance of valuing, mentoring, and empowering followers."[11]

The central assumption in transformational leadership is the shift from a focus on great leaders (or a leader-centered approach) and a transactional approach to interactional or collaborative leadership which emphasizes relationship. For Burns, transactional leadership is a leadership praxis focused on an "exchange [of] one thing for another" while transformational leadership is mainly about looking for "potential motives in followers [and] to satisfy [their] higher needs [by engaging] the full person of the followers."[12]

At the core of transformational leadership theory is an emphasis on relationship. As Burns contends, "we much see power—and leadership—as nothing but as *relationship*."[13] As Burns argues, it is within the relationship of power that encompasses the needs and values of both the leader and followers that people are elevated to a higher level of moral development.[14] It is this aspect of transformational leadership that distinguishes it from other leadership theories that focuses on leaders as agents of change by disregarding "the possibility of persons experiencing deep change [in their relationship with each other and] in the process of doing their work and in return contributing newness to their organization."[15]

The research indicates that the studied EECMY congregations have adopted a communal leadership style whereby every member is given an opportunity to participate in all kinds of activities of the congregations.

11. Echols, "Transformational/Servant Leadership," 98. Skip Bell also describes transformational leadership as a development process which involves integration of learning, changing, and doing. The outcome of this process is formation and empowerment of emerging leaders who themselves become the means for others to grow as leaders. See Beli, "Learning, Changing, and Doing," 93.

12. Burns, *Leadership*, 4.

13. Burns, *Leadership*, 4.

14. I Burns, *Leadership*, 41–43.

15. Beli, "Learning, Changing, and Doing," 93.

Members participate in all activities except administration of sacraments (which is considered the duty of ordained ministers). Transformational leadership, in the EECMY context, is not simply something that is experienced between a leader and his/her follows, but within the relationship or interaction of people working together as a group or a community.

The communal leadership practices of the EECMY congregations are similar to what Burns describe as the focus of transformational leadership. For Burns, transformational leadership is experienced in organizational interactions. In other words, "such leadership occurs when one or more persons engage with others in such a way that leaders and followers raise one another to a higher level of motivation and morality. Their purpose becomes fused. Power bases are linked not as counterweights but as mutual support for common purpose."[16]

The research also shows that the other form or level of personal experience that leads to formation of members as leaders is engaging the public holistically. Members of the studied EECMY congregations have confirmed that emerging leaders are formed and empowered in the process of engaging the needs of their community. This is similar to what Burns describe as the experience of those that emerged as transformational leaders such as Lenin, Mao, and Gandhi while engaging the needs of their public followers.[17] This is the reason why Burns refers to transformational leadership as "a socialized leadership"—a leadership "concerned with [meeting the demands or] collective good" of others (or the public).[18]

This is similar to what Burns describe as the experience of those that emerged as transformational leaders such as Lenin, Mao, and Gandhi while engaging the needs of their public followers.[19] This is the reason why Burns refers to transformational leadership as "a socialized leadership"—a leadership "concerned with [meeting the demands or] collective good" of others (or the public).[20]

16. Burns, *Leadership*, 20.

17. Burns, *Leadership*, 129–130, 137, 252–254.

18. Burns, *Leadership*, 173.

19. Burns, *Leadership*, 129–130, 137, 252–254.

20. Burns, *Leadership*, 173.

SIGNIFICANCE OF THE RESEARCH

J.K. Mugambi describes a Christian theology developed in the African context as "the discourse which is being conducted by Africans, in order to relate their own cultural and religious heritage to Christianity."[21] It is the study of cultures of African congregations that enables us to understand and articulate theologies that are being developed from African perspectives. As Nicholas Healy rightly articulates, "by thinking and acting as Christians," congregations are "already in some sense engaged in the practice of theology, whether [they] actually engage in critical reflection upon [their] lives as Christians or not."[22] Doing theology requires "attentiveness to specific people doing specific things together within a specific frame of shared meaning."[23] This leads us to conclude that it is impossible to dissociate theology from congregations. And it is the work of theologians to help these congregations be able to articulate the theologies that are being practiced.

According to Mbiti, Christian theology in an African context has various forms: namely, oral, symbolic, and written. By written theology, he means the contributions of a few Christian theologians "who have had considerable education and who generally articulate their theological reflections in articles and books."[24] Oral theology results from the masses, through vernacular languages, song, sermon, teaching, prayer, conversation, and so on. Symbolic theology is "expressed through art, sculpture, drama, symbols, rituals, dance, colors, numbers, and so on."[25]

As the research shows, the theology and practice of all four studied congregations are shaped by African cultural values. The way they articulate their identity and practice, the cultures of the congregations, are shaped by indigenous cultural values. This is demonstrated in their use of cultural terms in describing their identity and praxis and how they worship and engage the public (see "theory of culture" above).

This study has shown that leadership formation is a complex process that involves activities that take place within a church as well as in public, and that the Christian community as a whole (not just the few assigned

21. Mugambi, *African Christian Theology*, 9.
22. Healy, *Church, World, and the Christian Life*, 2.
23. Volf and Bass, *Practicing Theology*, 3.
24. Mbiti, *Bible and Theology in African Christianity*, 46–47.
25Mbiti, *Bible and Theology in African Christianity*, 46–47.

or ordained leaders) have significant contributions to it. The culture of congregations determine how leaders are formed and empowered. When congregations adopt holistic approach to ministry, they create favorable environment for integrated leadership formation and empowerment.

This finding helps us reevaluate leadership theories that are focused on the influence of a leader on his/her followers or a "big man" leadership approach. It also helps us to consider the significance of considering a communal culture or shared leadership for leadership formation. More importantly, it highlights the significance of the public ministry of congregations for leadership formation. According to Simpson, what is missing so far in the missional church conversation is a public church and "a public theology dimension in a full-orbed way."[26]

As also previously acknowledged, very little has been done in studying theology from the congregation's perspective. Congregations have been recipients of theology developed in seminaries and Bible schools rather than serving as partners in doing theology. This research contributes to the few studies (in congregational studies) that have adopted an approach to developing theology by keeping the church, the academy, and the public in dialog. More importantly, this research emphasizes the argument that congregations should "become a primary location that helps generate theology. Such theology is the result of people reflecting on the lived practices of how congregations understand the Christian thing."[27]

This research also aims at initiating a missional church conversation in the African context, particularly in Ethiopia. As described in the introductory chapter, except for a few works which reflected on the writings of Alan Hirsch from African perspective (which was done in South Africa), African scholars have not made any attempt so far to engage this conversation.[28] Therefore, the finding of this research can provide opportunities for guiding new theological conversation.

26. Simpson, "Missional Congregations," 136, 142.

27. Keifert, *Testing the Spirits*, 16.

28. The work of Alan Hirsch is influential in Southern Africa as it is also in Australia where he started his ministry, in Europe, and America. See Niemandt, "Five Years of Missional Church," 397–413.

LIMITATIONS OF THE STUDY AND FURTHER RESEARCH

The leadership formation practice of the four EECMY congregations described in the theoretical codes (chapter 5) are specific to the context of the studied congregations and are unique to the perspective of who participated in the interviews. Therefore, one should be careful not to generalize. Rather, what the finding of this research invites us to do is to understand, value, and start a conversation around critical issues and new concepts raised with regard to the nature of the missional church and the integrated leadership formation practices that are unique to the African context.

The other limitations of this research are that it is focused on the Oromo-speaking members of the EECMY. The EECMY, however, is a church that serves more than eighty different ethnic groups. These ethnic groups have their own culture that are in many ways different from the four studied congregations. Therefore, examining the communalities and differences of these cultures and how emerging leaders are being formed across the country are left for future research.

In this research, the four congregations were also studied separately without considering the impact that the network or partnership of congregations might have on the culture and leadership formation praxis of the congregations. As Simson rightly reiterated, one of the main characters of missional congregations is their commitment as "public moral companions." This means, according to Simpson, missional congregations "participate with other institutions of communicative civil society to create and strengthen the moral fabrics that fashion a life-giving and life-accountable contemporary society."[29] Therefore, future research might also examine the cultures of missional congregations that work in partnership with each other and with other organizations in the community and their impact on the practice of leadership formation.

CONCLUSION

This study has sought to explore the cultures of the EECMY congregations as they strive to promote the well-being of the members of society, and how emerging leaders are being formed and empowered by these cultures. The missional church is a church engaged in the ongoing creative work of the Triune God with a purpose of restoring the whole man. Missional leaders

29. Simpson, "Civil Society and Congregations," 427.

are formed and empowered when they are engaged in this mission and contribute their share to promote the well-being of the community.

This research was conducted with an understanding that the EECMY's theology of serving the whole person or holistic ministry has implications for the praxis of leadership formation. As the research showed, congregations create a favorable environment for emerging leaders to be formed as leaders when they are engaged in the mission of the Triune God through serving the whole man by addressing the social, physical, and spiritual needs of the community.

Appendix A

1. What is the congregation's view of the church?

    (a) What is required to be a church?
    (b) What do members of this congregation think about regarding the identity of a church?
    (c) What cultural languages or images are used to describe a church?
    (d) What biblical stories or passages do you use to describe a church?
    (e) Why does the existence of a church matter to you and this community?

2. Tell me what you think God is doing in this community through this congregation and its individual members.

    (a) What are this congregation's contributions in this community (both within and outside the congregation)? How is this contribution influenced by faith?
    (b) Besides faith, how do cultures inform the contributions this congregation makes in your community?
    (c) Tell me a story about how congregational action brings change in the life of the community it serves.
    (d) Tell me how the activity of the congregation is related to its own identity as a church.

3. Why do you, as a congregation, care about your own community and the community at large? What motivates you?

    (a) What symbols, rituals, or metaphors are used to describe this congregation's life as a whole? How are they revealed?

(b) What cultural images of God and humanity, biblical stories, and church tradition are important in the community's work of this congregation?

4. As the congregation seeks to empower leaders, what is God's role?

(a) How are leaders raised in your congregation?

(b) How do the congregational life and identity shape or empower future leaders?

(c) Describe the role faith has in leadership development in this congregation. Has prayer or Bible study had an impact?

In Conclusion

a. If we were to come back five years from now, what do you hope we find here?

b. Have we missed anything about the ministry of this congregation?

Appendix B

PERSONAL INTERVIEW QUESTIONNAIRE

1. How do you describe a leader?

   (a) What is required to be a leader?
   (b) What do members of this congregation think regarding the role and responsibility of a leader?
   (c) What cultural languages or images are used to describe a leader?
   (d) What biblical stories or passages are used to describe a leader?

2. 2) Tell me what you think God is doing in this community in forming and empowering leaders.

   (a) What are this congregation's contributions in the formation and empowerment of leaders?
   (b) Tell me a story about how congregational action brings change in the life of emerging leaders.
   (c) Tell me how the culture of the congregation is related to the formation and empowerment of leaders.

3. 3) As the congregation seeks to empower leaders, what is God's role?

   (a) How are leaders raised in your congregation?
   (b) How do congregational life and identity shape or empower future leaders?
   (c) Describe the role faith has in leadership development in this congregation. Has prayer or Bible study had an impact?

In Conclusion

(a) If we were to come back five years from now, what do you hope we find here?

(b) Have we missed anything about the ministry of this congregation?

Appendix C

INFORMED CONSENT FOR PERSONAL INTERVIEW PARTICIPANTS

You are invited to be in a research study of congregational cultures that results in the formation and empowerment of missional leadership. You were selected as a possible participant because you represent an important voice in this congregation. We ask that you read this form and ask any questions you may have before agreeing to be in the study.

This study is being conducted by me, Samuel Yonas Deressa, as part of my PhD thesis project in Congregational Mission and Leadership at Luther Seminary. My advisor is Dr. Gary Simpson.

Background Information:

The purpose of this study is to explore how cultures of congregations engaged in holistic ministry in the EECMY form and empower missional leaders. The study follows the rationale that there exists a correlation between cultures of these congregations and the nature of leadership.

Procedures:

If you agree to be in this study, we would ask you to participate in an interview about your lived experience of community within the congregation and how you see yourself being formed and empowered as a leader. Interviewees need to allow for two hours of uninterrupted time for each interview. The interviews take place in the pastoral office at the church. Each interview is videotaped and the researcher will also take notes.

Risks and Benefits of Being in the Study:

There are no risks to personal health or invasion of privacy involved in this study. There are no direct benefits to you, i.e. money, promotion, etc. as a result of this study. Indirect benefits to yourself/or the general public of participation are an increased awareness about how your cultural experiences and the life of the larger body of Christ results in the formation and empowerment of missional leaders.

Confidentiality:

The records of this study will be kept confidential. If I publish any type of report, I will not include any information that will make it possible to identify you. All data will be kept in a locked file at my home in Minnesota, USA; only my advisor, Dr. Gary Simpson, and I will have access to the data and video recording. If the research is terminated for any reason, all data and recordings will be destroyed. While I will make every effort to ensure confidentiality, anonymity cannot be guaranteed. Raw data will be destroyed by May 2018.

Voluntary Nature of the Study:

Your decision whether or not to participate will not affect your current or future relations with Luther Seminary and/or with other cooperating institutions, the Ethiopian Evangelical Church Mekane Yesus. If you decide to participate, you are free to withdraw at any time without affecting those relationships.

Contacts and Questions:

The researcher conducting this study is Samuel Deressa. You may ask any questions you have now. If you have questions later, you may contact me/ us at 2481 Como Avenue, St. Paul, MN 55108; or e-mail: sderessa001@ luthersem.edu. Phone: 651-621-9866. My advisor's name is Dr. Gary Simpson, and telephone number is 651-641-3253. You will be given a copy of this form to keep for your records.

Statement of Consent:

I have read the above information or have had it read to me. I have received answers to questions asked. I consent to participate in the study.

Signature
_____

Date
_____

Signature of parent or guardian
_____

Date
_____

Signature of investigator
_____

Date
_____

I consent to be videotaped

Signature
_____

Date
_____

I consent to allow use of my direct quotations in the published thesis document.

Signature
_____

Date
_____

Appendix D

INFORMED CONSENT FOR FOCUSED GROUP CONVERSATION PARTICIPANTS

You are invited to be in a research study of congregational cultures that results in the formation and empowerment of missional leadership. You were selected as a possible participant because you represent an important voice in this congregation. We ask that you read this form and ask any questions you may have before agreeing to be in the study.

This study is being conducted by me, Samuel Yonas Deressa, as part of my PhD thesis project in Congregational Mission and Leadership at Luther Seminary. My advisor is Dr. Gary Simpson.

Background Information:

The purpose of this study is to explore how cultures of congregations engaged in holistic ministry in the EECMY form and empower missional leaders. The study follows the rationale that there exists a correlation between cultures of these congregations and the nature of leadership.

Procedures:

If you agree to be in this study, we would ask you to participate in an interview about your lived experience of community within the congregation and how you see yourself being formed and empowered as a leader. Interviewees need to allow for two hours of uninterrupted time for each interview. The interviews take place in the pastoral office at the church. Each interview is videotaped and the researcher will also take notes.

Risks and Benefits of Being in the Study:

There are no risks to personal health or invasion of privacy involved in this study. There are no direct benefits to you, i.e. money, promotion, etc. as a result of this study. Indirect benefits to yourself/or the general public of participation are an increased awareness about how your cultural experiences and the life of the larger body of Christ results in the formation and empowerment of missional leaders.

Confidentiality:

The records of this study will be kept confidential. If I publish any type of report, I will not include any information that will make it possible to identify you. All data will be kept in a locked file at my home in Minnesota, USA; only my advisor, Dr. Gary Simpson, and I will have access to the data and video recording. If the research is terminated for any reason, all data and recordings will be destroyed. While I will make every effort to ensure confidentiality, anonymity cannot be guaranteed. Raw data will be destroyed by May 2018.

Voluntary Nature of the Study:

Your decision whether or not to participate will not affect your current or future relations with Luther Seminary and/ or with other cooperating institutions, the Ethiopian Evangelical Church Mekane Yesus. If you decide to participate, you are free to withdraw at any time without affecting those relationships.

Contacts and Questions:

The researcher conducting this study is Samuel Deressa. You may ask any questions you have now. If you have questions later, you may contact me/ us at 2481 Como Avenue, St. Paul, MN 55108; or e-mail: sderessa001@ luthersem.edu. Phone: 651-621-9866. My advisor's name is Dr. Gary Simpson, and telephone number is 651-641-3253. You will be given a copy of this form to keep for your records.

Statement of Consent:

I have read the above information or have had it read to me. I have received answers to questions asked. I consent to participate in the study.

Signature
_____

Date
_____

Signature of parent or guardian
_____

Date
_____

Signature of investigator
_____

Date
_____

I consent to be videotaped:

Signature
_____

Date
_____

I consent to allow use of my direct quotations in the published thesis document.

Signature
_____

Date
_____

APPENDIX E

OVERVIEW OF GROUP CONVERSATION PARTICIPANTS

Sours of Life Church

Participants	Age	Gender	Ministry
A	18-30	M	Youth ministry
B	30-40	M	Youth ministry
C	30-40	M	Youth ministry
D	40-50	F	Diaconal ministry
E	40-50	F	Diaconal ministry
F	50-60	F	Diaconal ministry
G	30-40	F	Diaconal ministry
H	50-60	M	Elders leadership
I	40-50	M	Elders leadership
J	40-50	M	Elders leadership

Family Life Church

Participants	Age	Gender	Ministry
A	20-30	F	Youth ministry
B	30-40	M	Youth ministry
C	30-40	M	Youth ministry
D	40-50	M	Youth ministry
E	40-50	F	Diaconal ministry
F	40-50	F	Diaconal ministry
G	30-40	F	Diaconal ministry
H	40-50	M	Elders leadership
I	40-50	M	Elders leadership
J	60-70	F	Elders leadership

Love in Action Church

Participants	Age	Gender	Ministry
A	20-30	M	Youth ministry
B	30-40	M	Youth ministry
C	20-30	M	Youth ministry
D	20-30	M	Youth ministry
E	40-50	F	Diaconal ministry
F	40-50	F	Diaconal ministry
G	50-60	M	Diaconal ministry
H	50-60	F	Elders leadership
I	50-60	M	Elders leadership
J	60-70	M	Elders leadership

Grace of God Church

Participants	Age	Gender	Ministry
A	18-30	M	Youth ministry
B	18-30	F	Youth ministry
C	20-30	F	Youth ministry
D	30-40	F	Diaconal ministry
E	40-50	M	Diaconal ministry
F	40-50	F	Diaconal ministry
G	40-50	F	Diaconal ministry
H	50-60	M	Elders leadership
I	50-60	M	Elders leadership
J	50-60	F	Elders leadership

Appendix F

IN VIVO CODES

Source of Life Church Focus Group Conversation

1. Community church
2. Mother church
3. Welcoming church
4. Healing ministry
5. Proclamation of the gospel
6. Sharing food
7. Sharing testimony
8. Worshiping community
9. Church founded on word of God
10. Bible-centered approach
11. Children ministry
12. Bible study ministry
13. Leadership development
14. *Waldaa Hadhaa*
15. Giving birth (planting) new congregations
16. Nurturing new congregations
17. Evangelizing communities
18. Members follow-up
19. Invitation to participate

20. Willingness to engage the community

21. Community culture

22. Mentored leadership

23. Listening to God

24. Congregation budget

25. Open church for the whole community

26. Counseling services

27. Women program

28. Women empowerment

29. Youth ministry

30. Outreach programs

31. Support to new congregations

32. Prayer service

33. Wedding services

34. Funeral services

35. Social services

36. Diaconal services

37. Mobilizing members

38. Developing projects for community services

39. Follow-up of projects

40. Assistance to neighborhood

41. Training service in the community

42. Raising fund

43. Clothing for the community

44. Sanitation project

45. Cleaning public areas

46. Advocacy ministry, voicing against domestic violence

47. Health ministry

48. Prophetic ministry of the congregation

49. Education on Christian responsibility in politics and economy

50. Serving the whole person

51. Living our faith, serving others

52. Confirmation class

53. Discipleship ministry

54. Ministers training

55. Formation of leaders

56. Culture of shared leadership

57. Women leadership

58. Participatory leadership

59. Vision casting

Source of Life Church Personal Interview, Pastor Mathew

1. Leadership as taking responsibility

2. Leadership as helping others

3. Leadership as achieving goal

4. Leadership as relationship

5. Common aspiration

6. Leadership in community

7. Church activities and leadership

8. Lay leadership

9. Pastoral leadership

10. Shared leadership

11. Decision making process

12. Pastoral office

13. Leadership practice

14. African traditional view of leadership

15. Holistic view of people

16. Leading worship

17. *Luba*, Oromo traditional leader, a pastor

18. Leader as a good shepherd

19. Servant leadership

20. Opportunity to serve

21. Priesthood of all believers

22. Fellowship of believers

23. Leadership formation and empowerment

24. Administration of sacraments

25. Children and youth ministry

26. Prayer group

27. Bible study group

28. Discipleship class

29. Gift of the Holy Spirit

30. Equipping ministers

Family Life Church Focus Group Conversation

1. Church as family

2. Spirit-led church

3. Church as community

4. Welcoming church

5. Church for the poor, offering hospitality

6. A mother church

7. School opened by the church

8. Church as home for the community

9. Church liturgy

10. Prayer for the sick

11. European song

12. Traditional song

13. African communal culture

14. Discipleship ministry

15. Evangelistic ministry

16. *Manaa ummaata,* home for nations

17. Discerning the Spirits movement

18. Offering hospitality

19. Care for members and the community

20. Seeking out people in need

21. Dig well projects

22. Women empowerment project

23. Open school for the community

24. A donkey project

25. Family ministry

26. Serving the whole person

27. Outreach ministry

28. Water pump projects

29. Medical services

30. Financial support to the poor

31. Starting small business project

32. Administer sacraments

33. Members participation in leadership

34. Leadership empowerment

35. Spiritual formation

36. Village programs

37. Bible study ministry

Family Life Church Personal Interview, Pastor Mark

1. Leadership as nurturing followers
2. Interpersonal skill
3. Leadership experience
4. Poor and marginalized members
5. Evangelistic mission
6. Holistic ministry
7. Cultural values of leadership
8. Envisioning the future
9. Prophetic ministry
10. Regular church service
11. Prayer programs
12. Bible studies in villages
13. Church projects
14. Leadership formation and empowerment
15. Spiritual formation
16. Women empowerment
17. Community service
18. Government workers role
19. Oromo cultural values
20. Lutheran heritage
21. Charismatic practices

Love in Action Church Focus Group Conversation

1. Outreach ministry
2. Budget for evangelistic ministry
3. Worshiping church

4. Traditional and contemporary worship

5. Church fellowship

6. Community service

7. Church as family

8. Church as community of disciples

9. Breaking of the bread and fellowship

10. *Waaqeffanna*, worshiping community

11. *Waaqeffatta*, the one who worships

12. Oromo traditional values

13. Public engagement of the church

14. Indigenous church

15. Social networks

16. Bible study programs

17. Prayer programs

18. Village programs

19. Enriching members

20. Mutual leadership culture

21. Praying for discernment

22. Health care ministry

23. Water project

24. Small-scale business project

25. Serving the whole person

26. Planting congregations

27. Healing ministry

28. Oromo traditional religion

29. *Waqaa ummaa*, God the creator

30. Leadership empowerment and formation

31. Spiritual formation

32. Participatory leadership

33. Enriching children and youth for ministry

34. Learning community

35. Lay leadership

Love in Action Church Personal Interview, Pastor Luke

1. Leadership and sense of call

2. Commitments to leadership

3. African understanding of leadership

4. Accountability to community

5. Shared leadership

6. Emotional support and affection

7. Good shepherd as a form of leadership

8. Servant leadership

9. Dynamics of socialization

10. Leadership formation and empowerment

11. Preaching of the work

12. Administration of sacraments

13. Outreach ministry

14. Fellowship of believers

15. Development activities

16. Evangelistic ministry

17. God in the life of the community

Grace of God Church Focus Group Conversation

1. Church as healing community

2. Church as reconciling community

3. Church as fellowship of believers

4. Loving community of people

5. Praying community

6. Participation in God's work

7. Help the needy, community service

8. Welcoming community of faith

9. Village programs

10. Bible study programs

11. Prayer programs

12. Community service

13. Spiritual healing

14. Serving the whole person

15. Traditional worship

16. Oromo traditional values

17. Contemporary worship

18. Music and art ministry

19. Evangelistic ministry

20. Planting congregations

21. Water pump projects

22. Educational assistance

23. Food and clothing for the poor

24. Community leadership

25. Leadership formation and empowerment

26. Discipleship ministry

27. Confirmation class

28. Youth and children ministry

29. Small group ministry

30. Women empowerment

31. Devoted leaders

32. Shared ministry and leadership

Grace of God Church Personal Interview, Pastor John

1. Sense of vocation

2. Leadership as relationship making

3. Leadership development

4. African understanding of a leader

5. Leadership as interpreting the context

6. Culture of decision making

7. Commitment to prayer

8. Devotional life

9. Listening culture

10. Community-building skills

11. Shared leadership

12. Transparency and accountability

13. Oromo traditional values

14. *Ungaafa*, elders leadership

15. Oromo traditional religion

16. Leadership formation and empowerment

17. God's involvement in leaders life

18. Community development

19. Women empowerment

20. Youth and children ministry enrichment

Appendix G

CONSENT FORM (TRANSLATOR/AUDITOR)

I,_____, translator or auditor, agree to maintain full confidentiality in regard all data Samuel Yonas Deressa related to his doctorial study on "Title." Furthermore, I agree:

1. To hold in strictest confidence the identity of any individual related to the data;

2. To not make copies of any data or media;

3. To delete all electronic files containing study-related documents from my computer hard drive and any backup devices.

I am aware that I can be held legally liable for any breach of this confidentiality agreement, and for any harm incurred by individuals if I disclose identifiable information contained in the data to which I will have access.

Translator's or Auditor's name (printed)
_____

Translator's or Auditor's signature
_____

Date
_____

APPENDIX H

DEMOGRAPHIC SURVEY OF CONGREGATIONAL MEMBERS AND PASTORS

Questions	Please circle your answers	
1. Are you male or female	Male	Female
2. How old are you	Less than 18 18-25 26-30 31-39	40-49 50-59 60-69 70 or older
3. Number of years in ministry	Less than 3 3-5 6-9 10-14	15-19 20-25 26-29 30 or more
4. Position held	Elder Choir Diaconal Evangelist Bible study coordinator	Youth ministry Children ministry Pastor Women ministry Other:
5. How many years have you been going to this church?	Less than 3 3-4 5-6 7-8	9-10 11-12 13-14 15 and more

BIBLIOGRAPHY

Abate, Eshetu. "Origins and Growth of Evangelical Christianity in Wollayta." B.Th Thesis, Mekane Yesus Seminary, 1980.

Ammerman, Nancy Tatom. *Bible Believers: Fundamentalists in the Modern World*. New Brunswick, NJ: Rutgers University Press, 1987.

———. "Culture and Identity in the Congregation." In *Studying Congregations: A New Handbook*, edited by Nancy Tatom Ammerman, Jackson W. Carroll, Carl S. Dudley and William McKinney, 78–104. Nashville: Abingdon, 1998.

———. *Studying Congregations: A New Handbook*. Nashville: Abingdon Press, 1998.

Ammerman, Nancy Tatom, and Arthur Emery Farnsley. *Congregation and Community*. New Brunswick, NJ: Rutgers University Press, 1997.

Anand, P. "Capabilities and Health." *Journal of Medical Ethics* 31 (2005): 299–303.

Anderson, Leith. *Leadership That Works*. Minneapolis, MN: Bethany House, 1997.

Aren, Gustav. "Evangelical Developments after 1910." Addis Ababa: Ethiopian Evangelical Church, 1983.

———. "Onesimos Nesib: His Life and Career." *EECYM Information Release*, 1981.

Arén, Gustav. *Envoys of the Gospel in Ethiopia: In the Steps of the Evangelical Pioneers, 1898–1936*. Stockholm: EFS Förlaget, 1999.

———. *Evangelical Pioneers in Ethiopia: Origins of the Evangelical Church Mekane Yesus*. Stockholm: EFS Förlaget, 1978.

Ashcroft, Bill, Gareth Griffiths, and Helen Tiffin. *The Empire Writes Back*. 2nd edition. London: Routledge, 1989.

———, eds. *The Postcolonial Studies Reader*. London: Routledge, 1995.

Aspen, Harald. *The 1995 National and Regional Election in Ethiopia: Local Perspectives*. 10 vols. University of Trondheim: Center for Environment and Department 1995.

Bahru, Zewde. *A History of Modern Ethiopia, 1855–1974*. London: J. Currey, 1991.

———. *Society, State, and History: Selected Essays*. Addis Ababa: Addis Ababa University Printing Press, 2008.

Bahru, Zewde, and Siegfried Pausewang. *Ethiopia: The Challenge of Democracy from Below*. Uppsala: Nordiska Afrikainstitutet, Forum for Social Studies, 2002.

Bakke, Johnny. *Christian Ministry: Patterns and Functions within the Ethiopian Evangelical Church Mekane Yesus*. Atlantic Highlands, NJ: Humanities Press International, 1987.

———. "Issues of Ministry and Theological Education in the 1970s and Today." In *Church and Society*, edited by Paul Hoffman, 57–85. Vol. 2. Hamburg: WDL Publishers, 2010.

Balisky, Paul. "Ethiopian Church and Mission in the Context of Violence." In *Mission in the Context of Violence*, edited by Keith E. Eitel, 225–36. Pasadena, CA: William Cary Library, 2008.

Barrett, Lois. *Treasure in Clay Jars: Patterns in Missional Faithfulness*. Grand Rapids: Eerdmans, 2004.

Bartels, Lambert. *Oromo Religion: Myths and Rites of the Western Oromo of Ethiopia, an Attempt to Understand*. Berlin: D. Reimer, 1983.

Bartlett, David Lyon. *Ministry in the New Testament*. Minneapolis: Fortress Press, 1993.

Bass, Diana Butler. *The Practicing Congregation: Imagining a New Old Church*. Herndon, VA: Alban Institute, 2004.

Bass, Dorothy C. *Practicing Our Faith: A Way of Life for a Searching People*. San Francisco, CA: Jossey-Bass, 1997.

Baxter, P. T. W., J. Hultin, A. Triulzi, and Paul Spencer. "Being and Becoming Oromo." *Africa*. 67.2 (1997) 322–34.

Becker, Penny. *Congregations in Conflict: Cultural Models of Local Religious Life*. Cambridge: Cambridge University Press, 1999.

Bediako, Kwame "African Theology." In *The Modern Theologians: An Introduction to Christian Theology in Twentieth Century*, edited by David E. Ford, 426–44. London: Blackwell, 1997.

Behling, O., and J. M. McFillen. "A Syncretical Model of Charismatic/Transformational Leadership." *Group and Organization Management* 21.2 (1996) 163–191.

Bekele, Girma. *The in-between People: A Reading of David Bosch through the Lens of Mission History and Contemporary Challenges in Ethiopia*. Eugene, OR: Pickwick, 2011.

Beli, Skip. "Learning, Changing, and Doing: A Model for Transformational Leadership Development in Religious and Non-Profit Organizations." *Journal of Religous Leadership* 9.1 (2010) 93–111.

Bennis, Warren. "Leading from the Grass Roots." In *The Leaders of the Future,* edited by Frances Hesselbein et. al., 19-24. San Francisco: Jossey-Bass, 1996.

Bennison, Charles E., Kortright Davis, Adair T. Lummis, and Paula D. Nesbitt. *Praise of Congregations: Leadership in the Local Church Today*. Cambridge, MA: Cowley, 1999.

Bhabha, Homi. "Difference, Discrimination, and the Discourse of Colonialism." In *The Politics of Theory*, edited by F. Barker, P. Hulme, M. Iversen and D. Loxley, 194–211. Colchester: University of Essex Press, 1983.

———. *Nation and Narration*. London: Routledge, 1990.

Bingaman, Brock. *All Things New: The Trinitarian Nature of the Human Calling in Maximus the Confessor and Jürgen Moltmann*. Princeton Theological Monograph Series 213. Eugene, OR: Pickwick, 2014.

Birri, Debela. *Divine Plan Unfolding: The Story of Ethiopian Evangelical Church Bethel*. Minneapolis, MN: Lutheran University Press, 2014.

Blackwood, Vernon. "Historical and Theological Foundations of Paulo Freire's Educational Praxis." *Trinity Journal* 8.1 (1987).

Blauw, Johannes. *The Missionary Nature of the Church: A Survey of the Biblical Theology of Mission*. New York: McGraw-Hill, 1962.

Boff, Leonardo. *Trinity and Society*. Maryknoll: Orbis Books, 1988.

Bosch, David Jacobus. *Transforming Mission: Paradigm Shifts in Theology of Mission*. New York: Orbis Books, 1991.

BIBLIOGRAPHY

Branson, Mark Lau, and Juan Francisco Martínez. *Churches, Cultures and Leadership: A Practical Theology of Congregations and Ethnicities*. Downers Grove, IL: IVP Academic, 2011.

Braukämper, Ulrich. *Geschichte Der Hadiya Süd-Äthiopiens: Von D. Anfängen Bis Zur Revolution 1974*. Wiesbaden: Steiner, 1980.

———. "Historicizing Sacrificial and Initiatory Systems in Ethiopia." *The Journal of African History* 45.1 (2004) 173–74.

Browning, Don S. *A Fundamental Practical Theology: Descriptive and Strategic Proposals*. Minneapolis, MN: Fortress, 1991.

Brueggemann, Walter. *The Prophetic Imagination*. Philadelphia: Fortress, 1978.

Bujo, Bénézet. *African Theology in Its Social Context*. Maryknoll, NY: Orbis, 1992.

Bujo, Bénézet, and Juvénal Ilunga Muya. *African Theology in the 21st Century: The Contribution of the Pioneers*. 3 vols. Nairobi: Paulines Publications Africa, 2003.

Bulatovich, A. K., Richard Seltzer, and A. K. Bulatovich. *Ethiopia through Russian Eyes: Country in Transition, 1896–1898*. Lawrenceville, NJ: Red Sea, 2000.

Bulcha, Mekuria. *Contours of the Emergent and Ancient Oromo Nation: Dilemmas in the Ethiopian Politics of State and Nation-Building*. Cape Town: The Center for Advanced Studies of African Society, 2011.

Burns, James MacGregor. *Leadership*. New York: Harper and Row, 1979.

Nussbaum, Martha C. *Aristotle, Politics, and Human Capabilities: A Response to Antony, Arneson, Charlesworth, and Mulgan*. Chicago: The University of Chicago Press, 2000.

Callahan, Sharon Henderson. *Religious Leadership: A Reference Handbook*. Thousand Oaks, CA: Sage, 2013.

Cardoza-Orlandi, Carlos. "Postcolonial Insights for Religious Leadership." In *Religious Leadership: A Reference Book*, edited by Sharon Henderson Callahan, 731–35. Vol. 2. Los Angeles: Sage, 2013.

Carroll, Daniel. "The Bible, the Church, and Human Rights in Contemporary Debates About Hispanic Immigration in the United States." *Latin American Theology* 2.1 (2006), 161–84.

Carroll, Jackson W. *As One with Authority: Reflective Leadership in Ministry*. Louisville, KY: Westminster John Knox, 1991.

———. *Small Churches Are Beautiful*. San Francisco, CA: Harper and Row, 1977.

Carroll, Jackson W., Carl S. Dudley, and William McKinney. *Handbook for Congregational Studies*. Nashville: Abingdon, 1986.

Cavanaugh, William T., Jeffrey Bailey, and Craig Hovey, eds. *An Eerdmans Reader in Contemporary Political Theology*. Grand Rapids: Eerdmans, 2012.

Charmaz, Kathy. *Constructing Grounded Theory*. 2nd edition. Los Angeles: Sage, 2014.

Cladis, George. *Leading the Team-Based Church: How Pastors and Church Staffs Can Grow Together into a Powerful Fellowship of Leaders*. San Francisco: Jossey-Bass, 1999.

Clapham, Christopher S. "Rewriting Ethiopian History." *Ananales d'Ethiopie* 18 (2002) 37–54.

———. *Transformation and Continuity in Revolutionary Ethiopia*. Cambridge: Cambridge University Press, 1988.

Collicutt, Joanna. *The Psychology of Christian Character Formation*. London: SCM, 2015.

Conger, J., and R. Kanungo. "The Empowerment Process: Intigrating Theory and Practice." *Academy of Management Review* 13.3 (1988) 471–82.

Cormode, Scott. *Making Spiritual Sense: Christian Leaders as Spiritual Interpreters*. Nashville: Abingdon, 2006.

Creswell, John W. *Research Design: Qualitative, Quantitative, and Mixed Method Approaches.* Thousand Oaks, CA: Sage, 2003.

Creswell, John W., and Vicki L. Plano Clark. *Designing and Conducting Mixed Methods Research.* Thousand Oaks, CA: Sage, 2003.

Crosby, Robert. *The Teaming Church: Ministry in the Age of Collaboration.* Nashville: Abingdon, 2012.

Crummey, Donald. *Priests and Politicians: Protestant and Catholic Missions in Orthodox Ethiopia, 1830–1868.* Oxford: Clarendon, 1972.

Crummy, Donald. "Imperial Legitimacy and the Creation of Neo-Solomonic Ideology in 19th-Century Ethiopia." *Cahiers d'Etudes Africaines* 109.28/29 (1998) 13–43.

Cunningham, David S. *These Three Are One: The Practice of Trinitarian Theology.* Challenges in Contemporary Theology. Malden, MA: Blackwell, 1998.

de Alva, J. J. K. "The Postcolonization of the (Latin) American Experiance: A Consideration of 'Colonialism' and 'Mestizaje.'" In *After Colonialism, Imperial Histories and Postcolonial Displacements,* edited by G. Prakash, 241–78. Princeton, NJ: Princeton University Press, 1995.

Dearman, J. Andrew. *Religion and Culture in Ancient Israel.* Peabody, MA: Hendrickson Publishers, 1992.

DeGlaisse-Walford, G. Steve. *Mission as Holistic Ministry: Developing a Congregational Ethos of Community Engagement.* Georgia: Smyth & Helwys, 2008.

Deleuze, Gilles, and Félix Guattari. *What Is Philosophy?* . Translated by Hugh Tomilson and Graham Burchil. London: Verso, 1994.

Denzin, Norman, and Yvonna Lincoln, eds. *Qualitative Research.* Vol. 4. London: Sage, 2011.

Deressa, Samuel Yonas, ed. *Emerging Theological Praxis: Journal of Gudina Tumsa Theological Forum.* Minneapolis, MN: Lutheran University Press, 2012.

———. "Face to Face: The Ethiopian Evangelical Church Mekane Yesus and the Elca in Dispute a Time for Elevated Discourse." *Word and World.* 34.2 (2014) 200–202.

Donaldson, Laura. "Postcolonialism and Biblical Reading: An Introduction." In *Colonialism and Scriptural Reading,* edited by Laura Donaldson and R. S. Sugirtharajah, 10–12. Atlanta, GA: Scholars Press, 1996.

Donham, Donald L. *Marxist Modern: An Ethnographic History of the Ethiopian Revolution.* Berkeley, CA: University of California Press, 1999.

Donham, Donald L., and Wendy James. *The Southern Marches of Imperial Ethiopia: Essays in History and Social Anthropology.* Cambridge: Cambridge University Press, 1986.

Doornenbal, R. J. A. *Crossroads: An Exploration of the Emerging-Missional Conversation with a Special Focus on "Missional Leadership" and Its Challenges for Theological Education.* Delft: Eburon, 2012.

Drath, Wilfred. *The Deep Blue See: Rethinking the Source of Leadership.* San Francisco: Jossey-Bass, 2001.

Dudley, Carl S. *Basic Steps toward Community Ministry: Guidelines and Models in Action.* Washington, DC: Alban Institute, 1991.

Dudley, Carl S. *Civil Investing by Religious Institutions: How Churches Launch New Community Ministries.* Indianapolis, IN: Indiana University Center on Philanthropy, 1997.

Dudley, Carl S., and Sally A. Johnson. *Energizing the Congregation: Images that Shape Your Church's Ministry.* Louisville, KY: Westminster John Knox, 1993.

BIBLIOGRAPHY

Echols, Steve. "Transformational/Servant Leadership: A Potential Synergism for an Inclusive Leadership Style." *Journal of Religious Leadership* 8.2 (2009) 85–116.

Edgell, Penny. *Congregations in Conflict: Cultural Models of Local Religious Life.* Cambridge: Cambridge University Press, 1999.

Eide, Øyvind. "Gudina Tumsa: The Voice of an Ethiopian Prophet." *Svensk Missions Tidskrift* 89.3 (2001) 291–321.

———. "Integral Human Development." In *The Life and Ministry of Gudina Tumsa*, edited by Paul E. Hoffman, 37–76. Vol. 2. Hamburg: WDL Publishers, 2008.

———. "Political Dynamics in the Wake of Missionary Efforts within the Realm of Human Rights: The Case of Ethiopia." *Swedish Missiological Themes* 89.4 (2001) 473–85.

———. *Revolution and Religion in Ethiopia: The Growth and Persecution of the Mekane Yesus Church, 1974–85.* Oxford: J. Currey, 2000.

Elton, Terri. "Charactoristics of Congregations That Empower Missional Leadership: A Lutheran Voice." In *The Missional Church and Leadership Formation: Helping Congregations Develop Leadership Capacity*, edited by Craig Van Gelder, 175–208. Grand Rapids: Eerdmans, 2009.

Engen, Charles Edward van. *God's Missionary People: Rethinking the Purpose of the Local Church.* Grand Rapids: Baker, 1991.

Erlikh, Hagai. *Ethiopia and the Challenge of Independence.* Boulder, CO: L. Rienner, 1986.

Eshete, Tibebe. *The Evangelical Movement in Ethiopia: Resistance and Resilience.* Waco, TX: Baylor University Press, 2009.

Estrada, Nelson P. *From Followers to Leaders: The Apostles in the Ritual of Status Transformation in Acts 1–2.* New York: T&T Clark, 2004.

Christian Scharen, ed. *Explorations in Ecclesiology and Ethnography.* Grand Rapids: Eerdmans, 2012.

Fiddes, Paul. "Ecclesiology and Ethnography: Two Disciplines, Two Worlds?" In *Perspectives on Ecclesiology and Ethnography, Studies in Ecclesiology and Ethnography* edited by Pete Ward, 13–35. Grand Rapids: Eerdmans, 2011.

Fiedler, F. E. *A Theory of Leadership Effectiveness.* New York: McGraw-Hill, 1967.

Florian, L. "How Can Capability Theory Contribute to Understandng Provision for People with Learning Difficulties?". *Prospero* 14 (2008) 24–33.

Forslund, Eskil. *The Word of God in Ethiopian Tongues: Rhetorical Features in the Preaching of the Ethiopian Evangelical Church Mekane Yesus.* Uppsala: Uppsala University, 1993.

Fukui, Katsuyoshi, and John Markakis. *Ethnicity and Conflict in the Horn of Africa.* Eastern African Studies. London James Currey, 1994.

Gallagher, Robert L., and Paul Hertig. *Mission in Acts: Ancient Narratives in Contemporary Context.* Maryknoll, NY: Orbis, 2004.

Gebissa, Ezekiel "The Eecmy between Indigeniety and Globalism: Re-Measuring Growth, Re-Visioning Mission, Recasting Leadership." In *Theological Praxis: Journal of Gudina Tumsa Theological Forum*, edited by Samuel Deressa, 75–107. Vol. 2. Minneapolis, MN: Lutheran University Press, 2012.

Geertz, Clifford. *Deep Play: Notes on the Balinese Cockfight.* Bobbs-Merrill Reprint Series in Anthropology. Indianapolis, IN: Bobbs-Merrill, 1972.

———. *The Interpretation of Cultures: Selected Essays.* New York: Basic, 1973.

———. "Religion as a Cultural System." In *Anthropological Approaches to the Study of Religion*, edited by M. Banton, 1–44. London: Tavistock, 1966.

Gemechu, Olana. "A Church under Challenge: The Socio-Economic and Political Involvement of the Ethiopian Evangelical Church Mekane Yesus." Ph.D dissertation, Berlin University, 2006.

Getatchew, Haile, Aasulv Lande, and Samuel Rubenson, eds. *The Missionary Factor in Ethiopia: Papers from a Symposium on the Impact of European Missions on Ethiopian Society, Lund University, August 1996*. New York: P. Lang, 1998.

Gibbs, Eddie. *Leadership Next: Changing Leaders in a Changing Culture*. Downers Grove, IL: InterVarsity Press, 2005.

Gidada, Negaso, and Donald Crummey. *The Introduction and Expansion of Orthodox Christianity in Qélém Awraja, Western Wälläga, from About 1886 to 1941*. Addis Ababa: Addis Ababa University, 1972.

———. "The Introduction and Expansion of Orthodox Christianity in Qélém Awraja, Western Wälläga, from About 1886 to 1941." *Journal of Ethiopian Studies* 10.1 (1972) 103–12.

Gilkes, Patrick. *The Dying Lion: Feudalism and Modernization in Ethiopia*. New York: St. Martin's, 1975.

Green, Clifford J. *Bonhoeffer: A Theology of Sociality*. Grand Rapids: Eerdmans, 1999.

Greenman, Jeffery. "Spiritual Formation in Theological Perspective: Classic Issues, Contemporary Challenges." In *Life in the Spirit: Spiritual Formation in Theological Perspective* edited by Jeffrey Greenman and George Kalantzis, 23–35. Downers Grove, IL: IVP Academic, 2010.

Grenstedt, Staffan. *Ambaricho and Shonkolla: From Local Independent Church to the Evangelical Mainstream in Ethiopia, the Origins of the Mekane Yesus Church in Kambata Hadiya*. Uppsala: Uppsala University, 2000.

Gritsch, Eric, and Robert Jenson. *Lutheranism: The Theological Movement and Its Confessional Writings*. Philadelphia: Fortress, 1976.

Guder, Darrell L. *Called to Witness: Doing Missional Theology*. The Gospel and Our Culture Series. Grand Rapids: Eerdmans, 2015.

Guder, Darrell L., and Lois Barrett. *Missional Church: A Vision for the Sending of the Church in North America*. Grand Rapids: Eerdmans, 1998.

Guinness, Os. *The Call: Finding and Fulfilling the Central Purpose of Your Life*. Nashville: Word, 1998.

Gunton, Colin E. *The Promise of Trinitarian Theology*. Edinburgh: T&T Clark, 1991.

Gurmessa, Fakadu. *Evangelical Faith Movement in Ethiopia: Origins and Establishment of the Ethiopian Evangelical Church Mekane Yesus*. Edited by Ezekiel Gebissa. Minneapolis, MN: Lutheran University Press, 2009.

Guta, Megersa. "A Reflection Paper on the 1972 Eecmy Letter: 'On the Interrelation between Proclamation of the Gospel and Human Development'." In *Serving the Whole Person: The Practice and Understanding of Diakonia with the Lutheran Communion*, edited by Kjell Nordstokke, 183–206. Minneapolis: Lutheran University Press, 2009.

Haberland, Eike. "Notes on the History of Southern Peoples." In *Colloque Internationale sur Les Languagues Couchitiques*. Paris, 1975.

Hadaway, C. Kirk. *Behold I Do a New Thing: Transforming Communities of Faith*. Cleveland, OH: Pilgrim, 2001.

Haile, Selassie, and Edward Ullendorff. *My Life and Ethiopia's Progress, 1892–1937: The Autobiography of Emperor Haile Sellassie I*. Oxford: Oxford University Press, 1976.

Hall, Stuart. "When Was 'the Post-Colonial'? Thinking at the Limit." In *The Post-Colonial Question: Common Skies*, edited by Iain Chambers and Lidia Curti, 242–60. London: Routledge, 1996.

Hamer, John. *Humane Development: Participation and Change among the Sadama of Ethiopia*. Tuscaloosa: The University of Alabama Press, 1987.

Hassen, Mohammed. *The Oromo of Ethiopia a History, 1570–1860*. Cambridge: Cambridge University Press, 1990.

Healy, Nicholas M. *Church, World, and the Christian Life: Practical-Prophetic Ecclesiology*. Cambridge Studies in Christian Doctrine. Vol. 7. Cambridge: Cambridge University Press, 2000.

Helland, Roger, and Leonard Hjalmarson. *Missional Spirituality: Embodying God's Love from the inside Out*. Downers Grove, IL: InterVarsity, 2011.

Hellen, Tiffin, ed. *Introduction, Past the Last Lost: Theorizing Post-Colonialism and Post-Modernism*. Calgary: University of Calgary Press, 1990.

Hendriks, H. Jurgens. *Studying Congregations in Africa*. Wellington, South Africa: Shumani, 2004.

Hess, Mary E. *Engaging Technology in Theological Education: All That We Can't Leave Behind*. Lanham, MD: Rowman and Littlefield, 2005.

Hirpo, T. "The Cost of Discipleship: The Story of Gudina Tumsa." *Word and World*. 25.2 (2005) 159–71.

Hirpo, Tasgara. "The Cost of Discipleship: The Story of Gudina Tumsa." *Word and World*. 25.2 (2005) 159–71.

Hirsch, Alan. "Defining Missional: The Word Is Everywhere, but Where Did It Come from and What Does It Really Mean?" *Leadership* 29.4 (2008) 20–22.

———. *The Forgotten Ways: Reactivating the Missional Church*. Grand Rapids: Brazos, 2006.

Hoffman, Paul, ed. *Church and Society: Second Missiological Seminar on the Life and Ministry of Gudina Tumsa, General Secretary of the Ethiopian Evangelical Church Mekane Yesus (1966–1979)*. Hamburg: WDL-Publishers, 2011.

Hofstee, W. "The Interpretation of Religion: Some Remarks on the Work of Clifford Geertz." *Neue Zeitschrift für Systematische Theologie und Religionsphilosophie* 27.2 (1985) 145–58.

Hoge, Dean R. *Money Matters: Personal Giving in American Churches*. Louisville, Kentucky.: Westminster John Knox Press, 1996.

Holcomb, Bonnie, and Sisay Ibssa. *The Invention of Ethiopia*. Trenton, NJ: Red Sea Press, 1990.

Hopewell, James F. *Congregation: Stories and Structures*. Philadelphia: Fortress, 1987.

Hunt, J., and J. Conger. "From Where We Sit: An Assessment of Transformational and Charismatic Leadership Research." *Leadership Quarterly* 12.1 (1999) 335–43.

Idowu, Bọlaji "The Predicament of the Church in Africa." In *Christianity in Tropical Africa: Studies Presented and Discussed at the Seventh International African Seminar, University of Ghana, April 1965*, edited by C. G. Baëta, 417–41. London: Oxford University Press, 1968.

Jaffero, Djalletta. "Ethiopianization and Missionary Personnel." In *For the Gospel and the Church: Documents of the Rev. Gudina Tumsa and Mekane Yesus Church from the Period 1961–1970*. Addis Ababa: Gudina Tumsa Foundation, 2006.

Jalata, Asafa. *Contending Nationalisms of Oromia and Ethiopia : Struggling for Statehood, Sovereignty, and Multinational Democracy*. Binghamton, NY: Global Academic, 2010.

————. *Oromo Nationalism and the Ethiopian Discourse: The Search for Freedom and Democracy.* Lawrenceville, NJ: Red Sea, 1998.

James, Nieman. "Attending Locally. Theologies in Congregations." *International Journal of Practical Theology* 6, no. 2 (2002): 198–225.

Jenkins, Paul "The Roots of African Church History." *Bulletin of Missionary Research* 10, no. 2 (1986).

Jesman, Czeslaw. *The Ethiopian Paradox.* New York: Oxford University Press, 1963.

Jodhka, Surinder S. *Community and Identities: Contemporary Discourses on Culture and Politics in India.* New Delhi: Sage Publications, 2001.

Johnson, Elizabeth. *She Who Is: The Mystery of God in Feminist Theological Discourse.* New York: The Crossroad Publishing Co., 1992.

Johnstone, J. "Technology as Empowerment: A Capability Approach to Computer Ethics." *Ethics and Information Technology* 9 (2007): 73–78.

Jonsson, Eskil. "Narrow Management: The Quest for Unity in Diversity." Ph.D dissertation, Dept. of Business Studies, Uppsala University, 1998.

Jorgensen, Knud. *Equipping for Service: Christian Leadership in Church and Society.* Eugene, OR: Wipf and Stock, 2012.

Kanno, Ayalew. "On the Oromo: Great African Nation Often Designated under the Name "Galla"." *Journal of Oromo Studies* 14.1 (2007) 117–46.

Katongole, Emmanuel. *African Theology Today.* Scranton, PA: University of Scranton Press.

Keifert, Patrick R., ed. *Testing the Spirits: How Theology Informs the Study of Congregations.* Grand Rapids: Eerdmans, 2009.

————. *We Are Here Now: A New Missional Era, a Missional Journey of Spiritual Discovery.* Eagle, ID: Allelon, 2006.

Keller, Edmond J. "The Ethnogenesis of the Oromo Nation and Its Implications for Politics in Ethiopia." *The Journal of Modern African Studies* 33.4 (1995) 621–34.

Kelsey, David H. *To Understand God Truly: What's Theological About a Theological School.* Louisville, KY: Westminster John Knox, 1992.

Kinyua, Johnson Kiriaku. "A Postcolonial Analysis of Bible Translation and Its Effectiveness in Shaping and Enhancing the Discourse of Colonialism and the Discourse of Resistance: The Gikuyu New Testament—a Case Study." *Black Theology* 11.1 (2013) 58–95.

Korten, David C. *When Corporations Rule the World.* San Francisco, CA: Berrett-Koershler, 1996.

Krapf, J. L., Ernst Georg Ravenstein, William Stevens, M. Lämmel, and Vincent Brooks. *Travels, Researches, and Missionary Labours During an Eighteen Years Residence in Eastern Africa: Together with Journeys to Jagga, Usambara, Ukambani, Shoa, Abessinia and Khartum, and a Coasting Voyage from Nombaz to Cape Delgado.* London: Trübner, 1860.

Kwok, Pui-lan. *Postcolonial Imagination and Feminist Theology.* Louisville, KY: Westminster John Knox, 2005.

LaCugna, Catherine Mowry. *God for Us: The Trinity and Christian Life.* San Francisco: Harper, 1991.

Lambie, Thomas. "Pioneer Missions in Ethiopia." *Bibliotheca Sarca: A Religious and Sociological Quarterly* 5.85 (1928) 7–21.

Larebo, Haile. "The Orthodox Church and the State in the Ethiopian Revolution." *Religion in Communist Lands* 14.2 (1986) 148–59.

Larebo, Haile M. "The Ethiopian Orthodox Church and Politics in the Twentieth Century: Part I." *Northeast African Studies: Incorporating Ethiopianist Notes Northeast African Studies* 10.3 (1987) 1–17.

Lartey, Emmanuel Yartekwei. *Postcolonializing God: An African Practical Theology.* London: SCM, 2013.

Latourette, Kenneth Scott. *The Great Century in Northern Africa and Asia, A.D. 1800–A.D. 1914.* New York: Harper, 1944.

Launhardt, Johannes. *Evangelicals in Addis Ababa (1919–1991): With Special Reference to the Ethiopian Evangelical Church Mekane Yesus and the Addis Ababa Synod.* Münster: Lit, 2004.

Legesse, Asmarom. *Oromo Democracy: An Indigenous African Political System.* Lawrenceville, NJ: Red Sea, 2000.

Lerner, R. M. *Concepts and Theories of Human Development* New York: Random House, 1986.

Levine, Donald *Greater Ethiopia: The Evolution of a Multiethnic Society.* Chicago: University of Chicago Press, 1974.

Lichtenstein, Benyamin B., Mary Uhl-Bien, Russ Marion, Anson Seers, James Douglas Orton, and Craig Schreiber. "Complexity Leadership Theory: An Interactive Perspective on Leading in Complex Adaptive Systems." In *Emergence: Complexity & Organization,* 2–12. University of Nebraska Lincoln Press, 2006.

Luther, Martin. *The Blessed Sacrament of the Holy and True Body and Bllood of Christ, and the Brotherhoods.* Edited by Theodore Bachmann and Helmut Lehmann, 45–73. Vol. 35. Philadelphia, PA: Muhlenberg, 1960.

———. "The Bondage of the Will." In *Luther's Works,* edited by Philip S. Watson and Helmut Lehmann, 5–295. Vol. 33. Philadelphia, PA: Fortress, 1972.

———. "The Freedom of a Christian, 1520." In *Luther's Works,* edited by Harold J. Grimm and Helmut Lehmann, 327–78. Vol. 31. Philadelphia, PA: Muhlenberg, 1957.

———. *A Treatise on the New Testament, That Is, the Holy Mass, 1520.* Edited by Theodore Bachmann and Helmut Lehmann, 77–111. Vol. 35. Philadelphia, PA: Muhlenberg, 1960.

Maimela, Samuel "Traditional African Anthropology and Christian Theology." *Journal of Theology for Southern Africa* 76.1 (1991) 4–14.

Marcus, Harold G. *Haile Sellassie I: The Formative Years, 1892–1936.* Berkeley, CA: University of California Press, 1987.

———. *A History of Ethiopia.* Berkeley: University of California Press, 1994.

———. *The Modern History of Ethiopia and the Horn of Africa: A Select and Annotated Bibliography.* Stanford, CA: Hoover Institution, 1972.

Markakis, John. *National and Class Conflict in the Horn of Africa.* Cambridge: Cambridge University Press, 1987.

Martin, Robert. "Congregational Studies and Critical Pedagogy in Theological Perspective." *Theological Education* 33, no. 2 (1997) 121–46.

Mbiti, John S. *African Religions and Philosophy.* New York: Praeger, 1969.

———. *Bible and Theology in African Christianity.* Oxford: Oxford University Press, 1986.

McKnight, Scot. *Embracing Grace: A Gospel for All of Us.* Brewster, MA: Paraclete, 2005.

Miller, Mary. "Transformational Leadership and Mutuality." *Transformation* 24.3 (2007) 180–92.

Moltmann, Jürgen. *The Church in the Power of the Spirit: A Contribution to Messianic Ecclesiology.* Minneapolis: Fortress, 1993.

————. *The Trinity and the Kingdom: The Doctrine of God.* San Francisco: Harper and Row, 1981.

Moltmann, Jürgen. *God in Creation: A New Theology of Creation and the Spirit of God.* The Gifford Lectures: 1984–85. San Francisco: Harper and Row, 1985.

Moltmann, Jürgen "Perichoresis: An Old Magic Word for a New Trinitarian Theology." In *Trinity, Community, and Power: Mapping Trajectories in Wesleyan Theology,* edited by M. Douglas Meeks, 111–25. Nashville: Kingswood, 2000.

Mugambi, J.N.K. *African Christian Theology: An Introduction* Nairobi: East African Educational Publishers, 1989.

Nahum, Fasil. *Constitution for a Nation of Nations: The Ethiopian Prospect.* Lawrenceville, NJ: Red Sea, 1997.

Nelson, Peter K. *Leadership and Discipleship.* Atlanta: Scholars Press, 1994.

Newbigin, Lesslie. *Foolishness to the Greeks: The Gospel and Western Culture.* Grand Rapids, MI: Eerdmans, 1986.

————. *The Open Secret: An Introduction to the Theology of Mission.* Grand Rapids: Eerdmans, 1995.

Niemandt, Cornelius. "Five Years of Missional Church: Reflections on Missional Ecclesiology." *Missionalia* 38.3 (2010) 397–412.

Noll, Mark A. *A History of Christianity in the United States and Canada.* Grand Rapids, MI: Eerdmans, 1992.

Norberg, Viveca Halldin. *Swedes in Haile Selassie's Ethiopia, 1924–1952: A Study in Early Development Co-Operation.* Uppsala: Almqvist and Wiksell International, 1977.

Nordfeldt, Martin. *Med Vagrojare I Gallaland.* Stockholm: Evangeliska Fosterlands-Stiftelsens Bokforlag, 1934.

Northouse, Peter. *Leadership: Theory and Practice.* Vol. 5. Thousand Oaks, CA Sage, 2010.

Northouse, Peter Guy. *Leadership: Theory and Practice.* Vol. 4. Thousand Oaks, CA. Sage, 2006.

Nouwen, Henri J. M. *In the Name of Jesus: Reflections on Christian Leadership.* New York: Crossroad, 1989.

Nussbaum, Martha C. *Creating Capabilities: The Human Development Approach.* Massachusetts: Harvard University Press, 2011.

————. *Frontiers of Justice: Disability, Nationality, Species Membership.* The Tanner Lectures on Human Values. Cambridge, MA: Belknap, 2006.

————. *Upheavals of Thought: The Intelegence of Emotions* Cambridge: Cambridge University Press, 2001.

————. "Women and Cultural Universals." In *Sex and Social Justice,* 29–55. Oxford: Oxford University Press, 1999.

————. *Women and Human Development: The Capabilities Approach.* Cambridge: Cambridge University Press, 2000.

Osmer, Richard Robert. *Practical Theology: An Introduction.* Grand Rapids, MI: Eerdmans, 2008.

Østebø, Terje. "The Question of Becoming: Islamic Reform Movements in Contemporary Ethiopia." *Journal of Religion in Africa* 38.4 (2008) 416–46.

Pankhurst, Richard. "The Role of Foreigners in Nineteenth Century Ethiopia Prior to the Rise of Menelik." Boston: Boston University Papers on Africa, 1966.

Pankhurst, Richard, and Thomas Leiper Kane. *The Ethiopian Borderlands: Essays in Regional History from Ancient Times to the End of the 18th Century.* Lawrenceville, NJ: Red Sea, 1997.

BIBLIOGRAPHY

Perham, Margery. *The Government of Ethiopia.* London: Faber, 1969.

Phillips, Thomas E. "More Than a Passover: Inculturation in the Supper Narratives of the New Testament by Fergus J. King." *Religious Studies Review* 34.4 (2008) 292.

"Proclamation No. 31 of 1975." *Basic Documentations of the Ethiopian Revolution.* Addis Ababa: Provincial Office for Mass Organizational Affairs, 1977.

Pui-lan, ed. *Postcolonial Imagination and Feminist Theology.* 1st edition. Louisville, KY: Westminster John Knox, 2005.

Rahmato, Dessalegn. "The Land Question and Reform Policy: Issue for Debate." *Dialogue, Journal of Addis Ababa Teachers' Association* 7, no. 1 (1992): 43–47.

Ramsay, J. Nancy. "The Congregation as a Culture: Implications for Ministry." *Encounter* 53, no. 36 (1992).

Richards, Larry, and Clyde Hoeldtke. *A Theology of Church Leadership.* Grand Rapids: Zondervan Pub. House, 1980.

Rivera, Mayra. *The Touch of Transcendence: A Postcolonial Theology of God.* 1st ed. Louisville John Knox Press, 2007.

Roxburgh, Alan J. "Missional Leadership: Equipping God's People for Mission." In *Missional Church,* edited by Darrell L. Guder, 183–221. Grand Rapids: Eerdmans, 1998.

Roxburgh, Alan J., and Fred Romanuk. *The Missional Leader: Equipping Your Church to Reach a Changing World.* San Francisco, CA: Jossey-Bass, 2006.

Roxburgh, J. Alan. "Missional Leadership." In *Religious Leadership: A Reference Handbook* edited by Sharon Henderson Callahan, 127–36. Thousand Oaks, CA: Sage, 2013.

Rubin, Herbert, and Irene Rubin. *Qualitative Interviewing: The Art of Hearing Data.* 3rd edition. Los Angeles: Sage, 2012.

S., Huntington. "Political Development in Ethiopia: A Peasant-Based Dominant-Party Democracy." *Report to USAID/Ethiopia on Consultations with the Constitutional Commission,* 1993.

Sæverås, Olav. *On Church-Mission Relations in Ethiopia 1944–1969: With Special Reference to the Evangelical Church Mekane Yesus and the Lutheran Missions.* Lund: Lund, 1974.

Said, Edward W. *Culture and Imperialism.* New York: First Vintage, 1994.

———. *Orientalism.* 1st edition. New York: Pantheon, 1978.

———. *Reflections on Exile and Other Essays.* Cambridge, MA: Harvard University Press, 2000.

———. *The World, the Text, and the Critic.* London: Vintage, 1991.

Salih, Mohamed Abdel Rahim M., and John Markakis. *Ethnicity and the State in Eastern Africa.* Uppsala: Nordiska Afrikainstitutet, 1998.

Samuel, S. *A Postcolonial Reading of Mark's Story of Jesus.* New York: T&T Clark, 2007.

Schech, Susanne, and Jane Haggis. *Culture and Development: A Critical Introduction.* Oxford: Blackwell, 2001.

Schein, Edgar H. *Organizational Culture and Leadership.* San Francisco, CA: Jossey-Bass, 2004.

Scherrer, Christian P. *Far from Oromia?: Ethiopia's Existential Antagonism Remains Virulent ; Analysis and Compiler of Interviews.* Moers: IFEK-IRECOR, 2002.

Schüssler Fiorenza, Elisabeth. *Democratizing Biblical Studies: Toward an Emancipatory Educational Space.* Louisville, KY: Westminster John Knox, 2009.

Schwandt, Thomas A. *Qualitative Inquiry: A Dictionary of Terms* Thousand Oaks, CA: Sage, 1997.

Scirghi, Thomas. "The Trinity: A Model for Belonging in Contemporary Society." *Ecumenical Review* 54.3 (2002) 333–42.

Scotchmer, David. "Symbols Become Us: Toward a Missional Encounter with Our Culture through Symbolic Analysis." In *Church between Gospel and Culture: The Emerging Mission in North America*, edited by George R. Hunsberger and Craig Van Gelder, 158–172. Grand Rapids: Eerdmans, 1996.

Sercombe, David. "Luke's Vision for the Church." In *A Vision for the Church: Studies in Early Christian Ecclesiology*, edited by Markus BockMuehl and Michael B. Thompson, 45–64. Edinburg: T&T Clark, 1997.

Sharan, Merriam. *Qualitative Research: A Guide to Design and Implementation: The Jossey-Bass Higher and Adult Education Series*. San Francisco, CA: Jossey-Bass, 2009.

Shorter, Aylward. *Toward a Theology of Inculturation*. Maryknoll, N.Y: Orbis, 1988.

Sider, Ronald J., Philip N. Olson, and Heidi Rolland Unruh. *Churches That Make a Difference: Reaching Your Community with Good News and Good Works*. Grand Rapids: Baker, 2002.

Simpson, Gary. "Africa Is the Lord's and the Fullness Thereof. Praise Be the Lord." In *So the Poor Have Hope, and Injustice Shuts Its Mouth: Poverty and the Mission of the Church in Africa*, edited by Karen L. Bloomquist and Musa Panti Filibus, 157–64. Geneva: Lutheran World Federation, 2007.

———. "Civil Society and Congregations as Public Moral Companions." *Word and World* 15.4 (1995) 420–27.

———. "God, Civil Society, and Congregations as Public Moral Companions." In *Testing the Spirits: How Theology Informs the Study of Congregations*, edited by Patrick R. Keifert, 67–88. Grand Rapids: Eerdmans, 2009.

———. "Missional Congregations as Public Companions with God in Global Civil Society: Vocational Imagination and Spiritual Presence." *Dialogue: A Journal of Theology* 54.2 (2015) 135–50.

———. "No Trinity, No Mission: The Apostolic Difference of Revisioning the Trinity." *Word and World* 18.3 (1998) 264–71.

———. "A Reformation Is a Terrible Thing to Waste: A Promising Theology for an Emerging Missional Church." In *The Missional Church in Context: Helping Congregations Develop Contextual Ministry*, edited by Craig Van Gelder, 65–93. Grand Rapids, MI: Eerdmans, 2007.

Simpson, Gary *Critical Social Theory: Prophetic Reason, Civil Society, and Christian Imagination*. Minneapolis: Fortress Press, 2002.

Smith, Kay Higuera, Jayachitra Lalitha, and L. Daniel Hawk. *Evangelical Postcolonial Conversations: Global Awakenings in Theology and Praxis*. Downers Grove, IL: InterVarsity, 2014.

Smith, N. Brien, Ray Montagno, and N. Tatiana Kuzmenko. "Transformational and Servant Leadership: Content and Contextual Comparisons." *Journal of Leadership and Organizational Studies* 22 (March 2004) 80–91.

Spivak, Gayatri. "Post-Structuralism, Marginality, Postcoloniality and Value." In *Contemporary Postcolonial Theory*, edited by P. Mongia, 352–63. London: Arnold, 1996.

Springs, Jason A. "What Cultural Theorists of Religion Have to Learn from Wittgenstein; or, How to Read Geertz as a Practice Theorists." *Journal of the American Academy of Religion* 76.4 (2008) 934–69.

Ståhl, Michael. "Ethiopia, Political Contradictions in Agricultural Development." Uppsala: Political Science Association in Uppsala, 1974.

Stebbins, Robert A. *Exploratory Research in the Social Sciences, Qualitative Research Methods* Thousand Oaks, CA: Sage, 2011.

Stewart, John "The Emergence of Congregational Studies in Oldline American Protestantism." *International Journal of Practical Theology* 6.2 (2002) 282.

"Strategic Plan Presented to the Eecmy General Assembly." Ethiopian Evangelical Church Mekane Yesus, 2013.

Strenski, Ivan. *Understanding Theories of Religion: An Introduction* 2nd edition. Oxford: Blackwell, 2015.

Sundkler, Bengt, and Christopher Steed. *A History of the Church in Africa.* Cambridge: Cambridge University Press, 2000.

Taddesse, Tamrat. *Church and State in Ethiopia, 1270–1527.* Oxford: Clarendon, 1972.

Tanner, Kathryn. *Theories of Culture: A New Agenda for Theology.* Minneapolis, MN: Fortress, 1997.

Teklu, Theodros Assefa. *The Politics of Metanoia: Towards a Post-Nationalistic Political Theology in Ethiopia.* Frankfurt: Peter Lang Publishing, 2014.

Tesema, Ta'a. "The Political Economy of Western Central Ethiopia: From the Mid-16th to the Early-20th Centuries." Ph.D dissertation, Michigan State University, 1986.

The Metaphysics Research Lab, Center for the Study of Language and Information. "The Capability Approach." *Stanford Encyclopedia of Philosophy.* https://stanford.library.sydney.edu.au/archives/win2016/entries/capability-approach/.

Thomas, Norman E. *Classic Texts in Mission and World Christianity.* Maryknoll: Orbis, 1995.

Tolo, Arne. *Sidama and Ethiopian: The Emergence [of] the Mekane Yesus Church in Sidama.* Uppsala: Uppsala Universitet, 1998.

Trimingham, J. Spencer. *The Christian Church and Missions in Ethiopia (Including Eritrea and the Somalilands).* London: World Dominion, 1951.

———. *Islam in Ethiopia.* New York: Barnes and Noble, 1965.

Tumsa, Gudina. *Witness and Discipleship: Leadership of the Church in Multi-Ethnic Ethiopia in a Time of Revolution.* Vol. 1. Hamburg: WDL, 2008.

Ullendorff, Edward. *Ethiopia and the Bible.* London: published for the British Academy by the Oxford U.P., 1968.

Unruh, Heidi Rolland, and Philip N. Olson. "Becoming a Church That Makes a Difference: Ventures in Holistic Ministry." Haddonfield, NJ: Interlink Media, 2006.

Van Gelder, Craig. *The Essence of the Church: A Community Created by the Spirit.* Grand Rapids: Baker, 2000.

———. *The Ministry of the Missional Church: A Community Led by the Spirit.* Grand Rapids: Baker, 2007.

———. *The Missional Church and Leadership Formation: Helping Congregations Develop Leadership Capacity.* Grand Rapids: Eerdmans, 2009.

———. *The Missional Church in Context: Helping Congregations Develop Contextual Ministry.* Grand Rapids: Eerdmans, 2007.

Van Gelder, Craig, and Dwight J. Zscheile. *The Missional Church in Perspective: Mapping Trends and Shaping the Conversation.* Grand Rapids: Baker, 2011.

Vaughan, Sarah. "Ethnicity and Power in Ethiopia." Edinburgh: University of Edinburgh, 2003.

Vaus, David De. *Research Design in Social Research.* Thousand Oaks, CA: Sage, 2001.

Bibliography

Virgin, Eric. *The Abyssinia I Knew*. London: Macmillan, 1936.

Volf, Miroslav. *After Our Likeness: The Church as the Image of the Trinity*. Grand Rapids: Eerdmans, 1998.

Volf, Miroslav, and Dorothy C. Bass. *Practicing Theology: Beliefs and Practices in Christian Life*. Grand Rapids: Eerdmans, 2002.

Wilhoit, James. *Spiritual Formation As If the Church Mattered: Growing in Christ through Community*. Grand Rapids: Baker Academic, 2008.

Williams, Patrick, and Laura Chrisman, eds. *Colonial Discourse and Post-Colonial Theory: A Reader*. New York: Colombia University Press, 1994.

Wimberly, Edward P. *Recalling Our Own Stories: Spiritual Renewal for Religious Caregivers*. San Francisco: Jossey-Bass Publishers, 1997.

Wuthnow, Robert. *The Crisis in the Churches: Spiritual Malaise, Fiscal Woe*. New York: Oxford University Press, 1997.

———. *Loose Connections: Joining Together in America's Fragmented Communities*. Cambridge, MA: Harvard University Press, 1998.

Wylde, Augustus Blandy. *Modern Abyssinia*. London: Methuen, 1900.

Yamamori, Tetsunao. "Serving with the Poor in Africa." Paper presented at the Africa Consultation on Holistic Ministry, Monrovia, 1996.

Yamamori, Tetsunao, Bryant L. Myers, and David Conner. *Serving with the Poor in Asia*. Monrovia: MARC, 1995.

Yukl, G. *Leadership in Organizations*. Upper Saddle River, NJ: Pearson Prentice Hall, 2006.

Zizioulas, Jean, and Paul McPartlan. *Communion and Otherness: Further Studies in Personhood and the Church*. New York: T&T Clark, 2006.

Zscheile, Dwight. "A Missional Theology of Spiritual Formation." In *Cultivating Sent Communities: Missional Spiritual Formation*, edited by Dwight Zscheile, 1–28. Grand Rapids: Eerdmans, 2011.

Subject Index

Addis Ababa, xi, 23, 54, 63, 64, 70, 71,
    85, 96, 106, 138, 173, 178, 179,
    181
Advocacy ministry, 129, 161
African traditional religion, 74, 102
American Lutheran Mission, xv
American United Presbyterian Mis-
    sion, xv
Apostles Creed, 32
Axial coding, 67, 68

Bible Churchmen's Mission Society, xv
Bible-centered church, 74, 116
Bible-centered worshiping, 74, 76, 77,
    124, 130
British and Foreign Bible Society, xv

Charismatic leadership, 52, 179
Children ministry, 70, 108, 160, 168,
    169, 171
Christian leadership, 11, 20, 31, 180,
    182
Church Missionary Society, xv
Community church, 81, 160
Community-building skills, 113, 169
Conference of Ethiopian Evangelical
    Churches, xv
Confirmation class, 73, 83, 162, 168,
Congregational cultures, 2, 6, 8, 9, 10,
    36, 50, 55, 56, 57, 59, 62, 69, 117,
    139, 151, 154
Congregational formation, 10
Congregational Studies, vii, 11, 13, 14,
    15, 16, 17, 18, 55, 56, 57, 144, 175,
    181, 185

Coptic Church of Egypt, xv
Critical Social Theory, 11, 41, 184
Cultural formation, 36, 37
Cultural studies, 14, 61

Danish Evangelical Mission, xv
Data gathering techniques, viii, 56, 59,
    60, 61, 64
Diaconal services, 161
Discipleship ministry, 74, 162, 164, 168
Doctrine of the Trinity, 26, 27, 28, 31,
    32, 35, 44, 118

Eritrean Evangelical Church, xv
Ethiopian Evangelical Church Mekane
    Yesus, xi, xiii, xv, 22, 23,
    152, 155, 173, 176, 177, 178, 179, 181,
    183, 185
Ethiopian Orthodox Church, xv, 86,
    107, 181
Ethiopian People Democratic Front, xv
Eucharistic fellowship, 33, 34, 36, 37
Evangelical Church Mekane Yesus, xv,
    113
Evangelistic ministry, 74, 87, 108, 109,
    125, 164, 165, 167, 168

Family Life Church, viii, xvii, 63, 85,
    86, 87, 88, 89, 90, 91, 92, 93, 114,
    120, 125, 127, 128, 133, 134, 135,
    139, 158, 163, 165
Federal Democratic Republic of Ethio-
    pia, xv
Focus group conversation, 62, 63, 64,
    68, 70, 71, 78, 86, 88, 102, 107,

Scripture Index